"As a beloved elementary scho[ ]
varsity football coach, Tony Le[ ]
the lives of literally thousands [ ] on
life and leadership. With To Lead a Good Life, Coach Legando
has now expanded his classroom and locker room to impart
those much-needed lessons on anyone fortunate enough to get
their hands on his book."

Ty Roth,
Random House Author

"Incredibly insightful, inspirational, and impactful! Tony's
words reflect a lifetime of leadership, character, and grit. His
significant legacy will live on through these stories, in addition
to the endless amount of lives he has touched along the way—
all enabling him to share his seasoned wisdom with us!"

Megan Casselberry,
Advancement Director,
Teen Leadership Corps

"I've had the pleasure of watching Tony Legando give a few
pregame speeches to his Huron football team, banquet
speeches, and plenty of post-game talks, some after victories,
and others following crushing defeats, but one thing was always
very clear--the man is a captivating speaker. This book proves
he's also a captivating writer, offering sound leadership advice
along with life lessons."

Dan Angelo,
Former Sandusky Register Sports Editor
and Assistant Editor of The College Store Magazine.
The trade publication of the
National Association of College Stores.

"Leadership is influence. Wherever you may work, live or play... you
have some degree of influence. Tony, a proven leader, has given us a
stirring inspirational and motivational tool to sharpen our leadership
abilities... to leverage influence. His stories, quotes and examples can
be life-altering for you and those you lead."

Jay Halley (DMin),
Team Pastor,
The Chapel
(Sandusky, Norwalk, Port Clinton)

"It might sound simple, but just imagine a room of people being inspired to do things the right way. Being driven to make the tough choices, not the easy ones. Tony Legando always had the power to do that through his speeches. Now he takes that ability and puts it into this book. Do someone a favor—get a copy of this book, and give it to them, especially if he or she is going through a tough time. It may just be that extra motivation he or she needs."

Allen Tittle
Founding Partner, Tittle & Perlmuter Law Firm,
former Huron Tiger Football Player

"I have had the pleasure of being around Tony Legando since my days as a young child, being able to see and personally experience the impact of these life lessons and captivating stories throughout his book To Lead a Good Life. This book gives everyone who did not have the opportunity of being taught or coached by Tony, the opportunity to divulge and be touched by his wisdom and astute mind. It will have a profound impact on the direction of your mindset and life."

Cody Thompson,
NFL Wide Receiver,
Seattle Seahawks

"Having the distinct pleasure of knowing Tony Legando as a coach and mentor for much of my life, his captivating nature and ability to motivate are unmatched. The life lessons learned from him in leadership, hard work, discipline and facing adversity are with me as a foundation in my own family and career. With To Lead a Good Life, Coach captured the spirit he brings with meaningful messages and lessons in written form. Highly recommended for those wanting to go deeper in their personal growth and development."

Stephen West,
Vice President,
AB Bernstein

To Lead a
Good Life...

A Wealth of Inspiration, Motivation, and Leadership

Tony Legando
Teacher, Coach, Speaker, Writer

To Lead A Good Life... A Wealth of Inspiration, Motivation, and Leadership
Copyright ©2020 Tony Legando

ISBN 978-1506-909-66-0 HCJ
ISBN 978-1506-909-67-7 PBK
ISBN 978-1506-909-68-4 EBK

LCCN 2020917725

September 2020

Published and Distributed by
First Edition Design Publishing, Inc.
P.O. Box 17646, Sarasota, FL 34276-3217
www.firsteditiondesignpublishing.com

To Pickles and Betty, my family,
and the students I've taught and coached.

Table of Contents

Part 1

Inspiration

Part 3
Motivation

Foreword

I first became familiar with Tony Legando through a mutual friend who also happened to be a young man who had played for him in High School. At that time, this young man was in the early stages of leading his own wonderful family, while also managing a highly successful career in the business world. Any time Coach Legando's name came up in our conversations, it was with the utmost respect and appreciation for all that Coach had taught him not only about the game; but more importantly, about life.

Years later when I finally got to spend some time with Tony, it became obvious very quickly, he truly was one of those rare coach/educators who not only understood the bigger why of his opportunities as a coach and teacher, but also walked the talk. In doing so, Coach was able to impact countless lives way beyond the field of play and the classroom for over 40 years as a football coach and educator.

THIS is why I'm so excited about *To Lead a Good Life...A wealth of inspiration, motivation, and leadership!* In a time where selfish motives and win-at-all-cost attitudes seem to rule the day, Coach Legando provides us with a welcome alternative to the norm as he shares his powerful insights on many of the leadership attributes that often seem to run against the grain of society today; and yet, need to be addressed now more than ever before. Empathy, integrity, perspective, and perseverance are just a few of the many topics Tony touches on in inspiring and impactful ways!

I've always felt the true measure of a coach or teacher is revealed through the lives of those they've had the opportunity to lead. And, as I shared at the onset of this foreword, I've seen first-hand how Tony Legando has

i

passed this test. Now, I'm thrilled that through *To Lead A Good Life...* Tony has given us all the opportunity to be encouraged and challenged by many of the same powerful and inspiring principles he utilized in his own journey of leadership as an educator over the years! I truly hope you will enjoy it, and gain from it as much as I did!

God Bless!
Todd Gongwer
Author *LEAD...for God's Sake!*

Preface

Being raised by a courageous father who was an amputee and an amazing mother who battled mental illness--as they raised eight, hard-working children--was a gift of inspiration and motivation. I cherish and appreciate their family leadership. How lucky were we to have Pickles and Betty show us how to get up early every morning, work hard, and battle adversity. They were living proof, with a little spirit, backbone, and grit, you can accomplish just about anything.

To be sure his family could attack the challenges of life, and stay creative in the process, my dad used to tell us, as only he could deliver, "Ya gotta give em a little razzle-dazzle." Because of a violent work accident, on one leg and three toes, the man gave us a little razzle-dazzle every day of his life.

To be sure we could all take care of ourselves and pursue our dreams, my mom gave us the love and affection necessary *To Lead a Good Life...* and keep up the good fight. Despite her own challenges, you couldn't ask for a more complete mother.

Growing up with 7 siblings, and having the privilege of watching them blossom, grow, and thrive was also a blessing. They home-schooled me on the intricacies of living life to its fullest.

My own family--all of them--could never fathom how much I respect their quest to reach their maximum potential. Through both thought and action, what I've learned from each about leadership, motivation, and inspiration, goes beyond comprehension. Their lead, follow, or get out of the way attitudes have given me the incentive to dig in, keep the faith, and make all my dreams of the heart. What more could a man ask?

The neighborhood I grew up in was the perfect place

for me to play ball, hang out at the beach, and rub elbows with a bunch of friends who knew how to have fun, compete, and appreciate the beauties of youth. Old Homestead was the perfect neighborhood for learning how to stand on your own two feet, hold your ground, and earn respect. We had it made.

In school, though I didn't apply myself much, my classmates, teachers, and coaches gave me an up-close and personal view of how a student should prepare for life's journey. As a teacher and a coach of over 40 years, I hope I had as much impact on my students and fellow teachers as they had on me. I've always believed teaching is the greatest of professions, giving me the opportunity to walk down the hallways and into the classrooms with some gifted people. What a wonderful educational experience I had and the pleasure was all mine.

Upon retirement, there was but one thing missing in my life: sharing what I've learned from others about influence, impact, and battling adversity. So here it is, I hope you enjoy reading *To Lead a Good Life...* as much as I've had in writing it.

Go ahead, turn the page, and get started in your quest to better lead, inspire, and motivate.

Acknowledgments

I would like to thank my wife Sandy for her love, encouragement, support, and patience throughout this process. Who has that much tolerance, strength, and understanding?

I would also like to thank my parents and my family for their love and inspiration throughout the years. Our journey together has been a godsend I've cherished throughout my life. You've given me the incentive to put pen to paper and create a work I hope we're all proud of.

To those people who graced the neighborhoods, the classrooms, and the playing fields I was fortunate enough to share my life with, thank you for enriching my journey. You gave me a reason to capture and write your stories of leadership, inspiration, and motivation.

To my editor Dan Angelo, how crazy were you to agree to work with an old coach who struggled to put two sentences together? I appreciate and respect your professionalism and fortitude. You deserve a medal!

To all those friends who read my first attempts at writing and didn't die laughing, I look back now and can't imagine what was going through your head when you read my work.

Ty Roth, your experience in the publishing process and your ideas in organizing the book gave me both the confidence and direction to put it together. Your help is much appreciated.

Mike Heydinger, your push was a blessing. Although I didn't listen much when I was a student of yours back in the day, throughout this labor of love you caught my attention and helped me find my way in writing *To Lead a Good Life...*.

Introduction

To Lead a Good Life... is a self-help book, featuring a personal collection of sixty-two motivational stories, inspirational essays, and lessons on effective leadership. From cover to cover, it offers unique examples of people with a little moxie, finding their strength, courage, and passion.

They are empowering stories of resilience, positive thinking, and overcoming life's challenges. Each story is designed to open the heart, strengthen the mind, and rekindle the spirit. In the end, this book is a tangible source of joy and comfort, encouraging its readers to strive, to thrive, to flourish, and *To Lead a Good Life*.

To Lead a
Good Life...

A Wealth of Inspiration, Motivation, and Leadership

Part 1

Inspiration

"To be inspired is one of the most powerful feelings known to man, a distant second only to inspiring others."
Anonymous

"Life is like a camera. Just focus on what's important, capture the good times, develop on the negatives, and if things don't work out just take another shot."
Author Ziad K. Abdelnour

"It's not the load that breaks you down, it's how you carry it."
Former College Football Coach Lou Holtz

"Hold fast to dreams, for if dreams die, life is a broken-winged bird, that cannot fly"
Poet Langston Hughes

"Those who say it can not be done, should not interrupt those doing it."
Chinese Proverb

"Out of the mountain of despair, a stone of hope.
Minister and Activist Martin Luther King, Jr.

1

To lead a good life...

Crank up the bulldozer and move mountains.

Ever notice, every child's a dreamer? Walk up to any youngster and ask, "What do you want to be when you grow up?" Without doubts, fears, worries, or reservations, they'll announce their intention of becoming an artist, a builder, a singer, a musician, a ballplayer, a superhero, or anything their little heart desires.

And they dream big. Real big. When they step to the plate with their worn-out bat, they don't dream about hitting a single, with a guy on third, to win a pick-up game in their own backyard. Nope. It's Yankee Stadium, a brand-new, Louisville slugger, with bases loaded and a 3-2 count. They proceed to hit a deep fly ball to center field. It's way back, over Babe Ruth's statue, beyond the scoreboard and into the parking lot. Yep. A walk-off home run.

And they have crazy imaginations. Hand them a piece of driftwood on the beach and it becomes a bulldozer. Without batting an eye, they move mountains, dig canals, or build moats around sandcastles built for kings.

And they have no fear. With bath towels tied around their necks, they'll leap tall buildings in a single bound. Not one-story buildings, skyscrapers, New York City skyscrapers.

Now, here's the million-dollar question: Why is it, as we grow older, many of us lose our fearlessness to dream, to create, to imagine? When did the angst, the doubt, the trepidation creep in? Better yet, can we get it back? Is it too late to compose our song, paint our masterpiece, or design the next Golden Gate Bridge?

Consider this: Laura Ingalls Wilder, author of *Little House on the Prairie*, was 64 when she published her first book. Some guy named William Ivy Baldwin tight-roped 320 feet across the South Boulder Canyon when he was 82, and astronaut John Glenn was 77 when he returned to space. They got it back. They kept their dreams alive. They proved, with the right fortitude and a little moxie, you can get it back.

We all know of Helen Keller. She didn't make excuses for her physical challenges. When she was 19 months old she became deaf and blind. With complete confidence and a strong will, she went on to become the first deaf and blind person to receive a Bachelor of Arts degree.

Romanian gymnast Nadia Comaneci didn't make excuses for her age. At 14 she dazzled the world, recording the first-ever, perfect score in the 1976 Olympics. Before she was done, she recorded 7 perfect scores and won 3 gold medals.

David of Goliath fame didn't make excuses for being an undersized, inexperienced, and ill-equipped underdog. As though a master soldier, he placed a smooth stone in his slingshot, aimed high, and hurled a devastating blow to the forehead of his king-sized opponent, knocking him flat on his back. As the biblical story unfolds, young David charged toward the fallen warrior and cut off his head.

Deep down, you know the drill: if it's important, you'll find a way. If not, there are a million, feeble excuses out there to lean on. As scientist George Washington Carver reminds, "Ninety-nine percent of the failures come from people who have made a habit of making excuses." And Founding Father of the United States Ben Franklin preached if you're good at making excuses, you're seldom good for anything else.

The next time you start to dream about leaping or bulldozing or hitting home runs, like old times, dream big. Tie that bath towel around your neck and leap, not one-story buildings but skyscrapers. Crank up that old bulldozer and move, not mounds but mountains. Or, heft that brand-new, Louisville slugger and swing, not for bloop singles but the fences. And who knows, with the right fortitude and a little moxie, maybe, just maybe, this time you'll hit it over the scoreboard and out into the parking lot. Go ahead. Have at it.

2

To lead a good life...

Focus on the roses, not the thorns.

How is it, some people facing the toughest adversities life has to offer, train their mind to focus on the good, the positive, and the productive potential in everything they experience? As though cut from a tougher cloth, with unwavering conviction, they understand their happiness, their lifestyle, and their future depends, not on the adversity they face but rather the quality of their thoughts.

President Abraham Lincoln, a master of simplicity and clarity, once remarked, "We can complain because rose bushes have thorns, or we can rejoice because thorn bushes have roses." Just out of college, I taught a young lady to drive. She saw nothing but the roses:

> *The vibrant young lady with the million-dollar smile had no legs. Despite her challenges, she realized life doesn't have to be perfect to be filled with happiness, joy, and laughter.*
>
> *Using metal crutches and a boat-load of determination, she lifted herself out of her wheelchair, allowing her father to gently guide her into the driver's seat. As she sat back and fastened her seatbelt, her smile broadened and her face came alive with teenage excitement.*
>
> *Her vehicle was equipped with motorcycle-like, hand controls attached to the steering wheel. With a burst of enthusiasm and complete confidence, she started the car, saying, "This is great! I'm ready to go!"*

> *Though the lesson was a challenge for both student and teacher, the results were encouraging. Impressed with the girl's resolve, and wanting to know more about her, I asked, "What are you going to do after graduation?"*
>
> *Without hesitation, she announced, "I'm going to college. I'm going to get my degree, get a job, find myself a good man, get married, and start a family of my own!"*

After just one lesson and one short conversation about her future, I knew how the young lady with no legs would react to rose bushes. There'd be no complaints about the thorns, she'd be too busy rejoicing the beauty of the roses.

Stephen Hawking didn't focus on the thorns in his challenges. Shortly after his 21st birthday, he was diagnosed with ALS, a form of motor neuron disease, and was given two years to live. Focusing only on the roses, Hawking forged ahead, becoming a celebrated physicist, author, lecturer, and professor.

At 13 years of age, it would've been easy for surfer Bethany Hamilton to see nothing but thorns. She lost her arm in a shark attack. Choosing a more positive mindset, she was back in the water one month later and won her first national surfing title two years later.

And Marlee Matlin knew how to focus on the roses in her challenges. She lost her hearing when she was a child. With the drive and determination of a soldier in battle, the actress and children's author went on to become the only deaf recipient of an Academy Award for Best Actress in a leading role.

Like Hawking, Hamilton, and Matlin, the passionate young lady with the motorcycle-like hand controls and the contagious attitude was also cut from a tougher, more resilient, more adaptable cloth. She realized her future depended, not on the demands of her adversities, but on the beauty, the quality, and the strength of her thoughts--all roses, no thorns.

3

To lead a good life...

Cause angels to sing.

Do you have a hero? I'm not talking about Superman, Superwoman, Batman, or his little buddy Robin. I'm talking about a real-life, non-cape bearing hero. If you do, take a minute, think about that person, and answer two questions. At first glance, does your hero appear ordinary? Looking a bit closer, has your hero, with extreme mental toughness and perseverance, made himself or herself extraordinary?

If the study of remarkable men and women has taught us anything, it is this: Heroes, of the mortal kind, come in all shapes and sizes, but there seems to be one constant running through their wondrous veins. They are ordinary people with extraordinary qualities.

Bob Riley, the 52nd Governor of Alabama, once said, "It is during hard times when the 'hero' within us is revealed." Terry Fox, the most famous non-hockey athlete in Canada, revealed his hero within after losing his right leg to cancer. A quick review of the extraordinary life and times of Terry Fox, in his battle to bring awareness to cancer, is summarized below:

> *Terry wasn't the type of young man to let adversity keep him down. He decided he was going to use his story to make a difference in the lives of fellow cancer victims, bringing awareness to the disease and raising money for research.*
>
> *To do so, he committed to running across Canada, from the shores of the Atlantic to the cliffs of the Pacific.*

> *He would run twenty-six miles a day, taking donations from anyone who wanted to support his cause. He called his journey the "Marathon of Hope."*
>
> *When he first dipped his artificial leg into the Atlantic Ocean, few people were aware of his intentions. Before he was done, word of the one-legged runner spread throughout the country. Huge crowds gathered to cheer the young man on and donate to his cause. He was becoming a national hero.*
>
> *After 143 days, 26 miles a day, and 3,339 miles--the equivalent of running from Miami to Seattle--the young man was forced to stop. His cancer had spread to his lungs, leaving huge growths and causing extreme fatigue and discomfort.*
>
> *Terry Fox passed away in June of 1981 at the age of 21. Today, statues of the hero fan out across Canada, each depicting the one-legged dreamer, running towards home. The young man who refused to let hard times keep him down, chose a path of character and class, revealing the hero within.*

As though written with Terry Fox in mind, American playwright August Wilson wrote, "Confront the dark parts of yourself and work to banish them with illumination and forgiveness. Your willingness to wrestle with your dreams will cause angels to sing."

With his attempted run across Canada, like a champion, Terry grappled hard and lit up the dark side of cancer. And though he couldn't complete the task, this ordinary young man with extraordinary qualities, caused angels to sing.

Born with one leg, Anthony Robles knew something about rejoicing success. Fit for a prosthetic leg when he was 3 years old, he was so self-conscious he hid behind the couch in his home.

Overcoming his fears, as a freshman in high school, Robles decided to wrestle. His first year, he was rated last in Mesa, Arizona. Refusing to give up, his training was intense. By the end of his sophomore season, the student with one leg, rated sixth in Mesa. Refusing to settle, he went undefeated during his junior season. Before he graduated, as though driven by a force from above, he won a state title.

Did he take his newly developed skills to the next level? Absolutely. He went on to wrestle at Arizona State University, winning the 2010-11, NCAA, national title in the 125-pound weight class.

There'd be no more hiding behind couches for Anthony Robles. And oh, how he caused the angels to sing.

By the way, if you're looking for an inspiring read, the National Champion authored a book entitled, *Unstoppable*--the perfect title.

4

To lead a good life…

Put blinders on and make a difference.

The most astonishing achievements known to mankind were directed by leaders who were tired and discouraged… but refused to give up. As if searching for oil, they just kept drilling.

Strong leaders share these three qualities of persistence:

- First, they have a willing heart, consistently reaching out to those who follow.

- Second, they have a positive attitude. As though wearing blinders, they stay focused, refusing to let negative influences control their situation.

- Third, they have a relentless desire to make a difference. Realizing you don't get much done leading only when you feel like it, they accept all challenges and work them hard… always.

As indicated below, some people develop those three qualities of persistence much earlier than others:

> *She was ten years old. Her mom and dad, consumed by drugs and alcohol, dropped her and her younger brother off at the local mall one cold and rainy evening. They never returned. Ever.*
>
> *Her teacher, watching this family tragedy play out,*

> *was impressed with the little girl's attitude. The student did all her school work, never complained, and stayed positive throughout the year.*
>
> *One day, he called her to his desk and said, "I'm very proud of you, young lady. I love how positive you are all the time."*
>
> *Her youthful reply, "Thank you, I have to stay positive, if I get sad, my brother gets scared."*

The young lady dropped off at the mall on that cold and rainy evening, though of tender age, somehow developed all three qualities of persistence. With a willing heart, she consistently reached out and showed her brother the strength he needed to see. As though wearing blinders, she stayed focused, refusing to let the adversity of abandonment control her situation. And finally, with a relentless desire to make a difference, she accepted her challenge, leading, not only on days she felt like it... but always.

Walt Disney, the man who spent a lifetime trying to awaken the youth in all of us, once said, "The flower that blooms in adversity, is the most beautiful of all." Had Mr. Disney met the young lady and watched her take care of her brother, he would've been impressed with the beauty of her persistence.

In working with young people for a lifetime, I would gather and share quotes with students gripped, squeezed, and sometimes smothered in the clutches of family adversity. There are three quotes on persistence that have served me well in guiding young people through family trauma.

The first is a Chinese proverb encouraging strength and stamina over the long haul, affirming, "Persistence can grind an iron beam into a needle." The second is by journalist and broadcaster Jim Watkins, who gained fame reporting on the September 11th, 2001, terrorist attacks. He proposed firm resolve over temper and force, saying, "A river cuts through rock, not because of its power, but because of its persistence." And the third quote was penned by self-help author Napoleon Hill. Offering hope, he said, "Failure cannot cope with persistence."

When someone on our team is troubled, it's our responsibility as leaders to find words of wisdom and use them to give guidance and hope, not only on days we feel like it... but always.

5

To lead a good life...

Tighten the bonds of friendship.

With warmth, a true friend peers into your eyes and feels your pain. With concern, they listen to your voice and hear the distress. Without asking, they sense a burden festering deep inside your gut. Bringing energy to the soul, there's a never-ending beauty in finding just one person in your life who can deliver those gifts.

Giving of themselves, with ease, a friend stands with you as one, taking on all struggles. And when the dark clouds pass, the bonds of friendship are tightened, leaving deep, personal rewards for both. As Italian philosopher and Catholic priest, Thomas Aquinas once said, "There is nothing on this earth more prized than true friendship."

The following passage, it's origin unknown, solidifies the value of finding someone who recognizes the hurt, the quiet, and the heaviness in your heart:

> *The teacher saw little Gracie outside the playground fence, standing alone near an old, red maple tree. Concerned for her safety, she hurried to the fence, telling Gracie to get back onto school property.*
>
> *As she approached, the teacher noticed a deep sadness in her eyes.*
>
> *"What's wrong, Gracie, why did you leave the playground?"*
>
> *Avoiding eye contact, she looked down and whispered, "Sometimes I feel sad because I don't have any friends. I feel like nobody even notices me, and I just want to be*

> *alone."*
>
> *"Gracie, I'll be your friend, and I'll help you find a friend. But I need you to promise me, you won't leave the playground again."*
>
> *As if her prayers had finally been answered, she said, "I promise, I won't leave again. And thank you for being my friend."*
>
> *Leaving school at the end of the day, the old, red maple caught the teacher's eye. Moving closer, she noticed a carefully folded piece of paper, wedged in the bark of the tree. Upon opening it, she found a short note written in near-perfect handwriting. It read, "If anyone finds this note, please, please, please, be my friend? With love, Gracie."*

Though the teacher struggled to find Gracie a friend, she stood with her each day on the playground, giving her a touch of strength and comfort. Before long, the pain in her eyes had calmed, the doubt in her voice found confidence, and the burden festering deep inside her heart, lightened with joy and laughter. With ease, the threads of friendship had been tightened, leaving deep, personal rewards for both. With new hope, there would be no more letters in the old, red maple--education at its finest.

Find the Gracie in your world, tighten the bonds of friendship, and feel the personal rewards. Why not? As Thomas Aquinas insisted, you'll find no greater prize on this earth.

Review: Stories 1 - 5

1
To lead a good life... crank up the old bulldozer and move mountains.
The next time you start to dream, like old times, dream big. Crank up the old bulldozer and move, not mounds but mountains. And who knows, with the right fortitude and a little moxie, maybe, just maybe, you'll fulfill those dreams.

2
To lead a good life... focus on the roses, not the thorns.
Some people understand their happiness, their lifestyle, and their future depends, not on the adversity they face but rather the quality of their thoughts. As Abe Lincoln once remarked, "We can complain because rose bushes have thorns, or we can rejoice because thorn bushes have roses."

3
To lead a good life... cause angels to sing.
Confront your fears. Illuminate them. Like Terry Fox, the most famous non-athlete in Canada who battled cancer, choose a path of courage, revealing your hero within.

4
To lead a good life... put on blinders and make a difference.
Strong leaders consistently reach out to those who follow. They have a positive attitude, stay focused, and have a strong desire to make a difference. Realizing you don't get much done impacting others only when you feel like it, they accept all challenges and work them hard... always.

5
To lead a good life... tighten the bonds of friendship.
A true friend stands with you as one, taking on all struggles. And when the dark clouds of adversity pass, the bonds of friendship are tightened, leaving deep, personal rewards for both. As Italian philosopher and Catholic priest, Thomas Aquinas, once said, "There is nothing on this earth more prized than true friendship."

6

To lead a good life...

Tie your shoestrings and find your own inspiration.

You want inspiration, take a walk. That's it! You won't need a compass rose, a road map, or a high-tech GPS system to guide your travels. Just put on your tennis shoes, open the front door, and start walking.

And here's a tip: As you travel through your neighborhood, make sure you stop, talk, and ask your neighbors a few questions about their life journeys and challenges. If you're sincere in your approach, you may find enough inspiration to last a lifetime.

Allow me to share a few examples of what I'm talking about:

> *I grew up in a small neighborhood, each street no more than three hundred yards long. In that neighborhood, and one street into the next, living within a few hundred yards of each other, were four men who played a significant role in World War II.*
>
> *Ted Temper was wounded in the Hürtgen Forest in Germany, fighting in the longest single battle the United States Army ever fought. With shrapnel lodged deep in his hip, he waited on the battlefield for medical assistance for over twenty-four hours. Mr. Temper lived just around the corner from my childhood home.*
>
> *In the face of horrific enemy gunfire, Roy Newsome was one of the soldiers storming France on D-Day, scaling the nearly impregnable cliffs of Omaha Beach with grappling hooks. Eighty percent of his battalion was lost in the first half-hour. Mr. Newsome lived one street*

> *into the next neighborhood.*
> *On June 6, 1944, Richard Klein parachuted into the night behind enemy lines in France. He was eventually wounded in the Battle of the Bulge--Adolf Hitler's last major offensive campaign on the Western Front. Winston Churchill called it "the greatest American battle of the war." Mr. Klein lived three streets away.*
> *Ken Bollenbacher was an aircraft carrier pilot instructor at Great Lakes Naval in Illinois. He was reassigned to go into the Pacific arena in 1945 and was one day out of San Diego on a carrier when the bomb was dropped on Hiroshima. Though he didn't actually fight in the war, he took great pride in preparing men who did. Mr. Bollenbacher lived one street away, directly behind my house.*

Though their personal accomplishments were never given much fanfare or marquee recognition, their life journeys are as powerful and inspiring as any of world-wide fame. Like those we read about in our history books, their stories of strength, courage, patriotism, and accomplishment will boost your spirits and warm your heart.

That's one small section of one small town. Imagine the stories in each town, waiting to be tapped, shared, and resourced. So, if you're craving some down-home inspiration, just tighten up the shoelaces and start walking. You'll find it.

7

To lead a good life…

Find a way to get back home.

I love this thought: "Home, though our feet may leave, our hearts never do." It's the place we dream of getting back to when we find ourselves lost in a world of cold, hurt, or uncertainty.

There's a yearning in all of us to open our front door, walk-in, sit down, and relax. Offering safety from the outside world, home is the place we can go and be accepted for who we are.

I'm not sure where I found it, but here's another thought I love: "Home is where our story begins, where we hang our hat and our heart." It's where our family and friends roost and blend, creating memories suspended in time, echoing a burst of laughter that never seems to end. Home is our little slice of heaven.

Here's what I've learned in my travels as an educator: to thrive, to develop, to succeed, and find happiness, we need support from home. To reach our potential and creative pinnacle, we need the warmth and security of a loving and nurturing family.

Imagine trying to rise above the clang and clatter of this crazy world without the comfort of a positive home environment. Oh, you can soar without it, but like a lone astronaut drifting off into space, the climb will be lonely and less rewarding.

When you find yourself in the grasp of distant chaos, how strong is the pull to get back home? Herein lies an answer:

One summer morning, as I was preparing to raise my United States flag, I didn't realize anyone was watching.

A bit later, my wife told me our neighbor was standing behind me, about 20 yards away. As if forged from steel, he stood at full attention with his right hand raised in salute. He never moved a muscle, until the flag reached its destination and was tied off.

I've often wondered what goes through my neighbor's mind when his country celebrates victory and honors its soldiers. He's a Vietnam veteran. More than 8,350 miles from home, he was a machine gunner in a UH1B transport helicopter. Their mission: transport the wounded and the dead, drop off ammunition, supplies, and replacements--sometimes in the heat of battle.

He did this job every day, for four and a half months. From 4 in the morning until 10 at night, he helped support and protect the troops in the Mekong Delta. Every day, that is, until he was wounded. The bullet pierced his shoulder, splintered his scapula, and busted a rib, leaving two holes in his lungs.

How strong was his desire to get back home? Follow this: After treatment, he volunteered to go back to Vietnam! Why? In his words: "In Vietnam, we were so busy, time went by much faster--made it seem I'd get home quicker. I just wanted to get home."

Though they refused to allow him to go back into battle, the two-time recipient of the Purple Heart, served out his duty in the states and finally headed home--that place he could hang his hat and his heart and once again blend with family and friends.

A touch late, and something our country didn't do very well back in the days of the war in Vietnam: Welcome home veterans. Thank you for your service. At full attention and right hand raised, we salute you.

8

To lead a good life…

Make all your victories of the soul and spirit.

Elie Wiesel, author, Nobel Peace Prize winner, and Holocaust survivor, once wrote, "There are victories of the soul and spirit. Sometimes, even if you lose, you win."

Mike Rowbottom, one of Britain's most talented sportswriters, shared the following story about a victory of the soul and spirit:

> *In Germany, in 1936, Jesse Owens was expected to win an Olympic gold medal in the long jump. The year before, he jumped 26 feet, 8 ¼ inches to set a world record, lasting an incredible 25 years.*
>
> *Walking up to the long-jump pit, he noticed an impressive looking athlete from Germany. Well aware of Hitler's desire for "Aryan superiority," the presence of this blond-haired, blue-eyed German, heightened the pressure on Owens.*
>
> *On his first and second attempts in the qualifying rounds, Owens stepped beyond the take-off board and fouled. Preparing for his third and final jump, the young German approached the American athlete, introduced himself as Luz Long, and offered some advice. He suggested putting a piece of tape on the board, a few inches from the edge, ensuring Owens would not foul a third time and disqualify himself.*
>
> *Owens followed Long's advice and it worked. He qualified and went on to win a gold medal.*
>
> *The first person to congratulate Owens, in full view of*

Adolf Hitler, was the man who finished third--the blond-haired, blue-eyed Aryan.

Though the German competitor didn't win the gold medal, in helping a fellow athlete, he found victory of the soul and spirit. Realizing integrity is not kept by winning at all costs, Luz Long chose to compete, not from within the parameters of Hitler's vision of a supreme race but rather from within the parameters of his own values, thoughts, and actions. For one brief moment, he set aside personal gain and did what he believed to be right, just, and of the heart.

Owens never saw Long again but in reflecting back, he said, "You could melt down all the medals and cups I have, and they wouldn't be a plating on a 24-carat friendship I felt for Luz Long." As the realities of Hitler's war would have it, Luz Long was killed in battle in World War II.

There's another, well-documented story from the same time period. It offers a tragic, yet uplifting example of victory through defeat. Eventually dying in a concentration camp of starvation and disease, Anne Frank lost her battle with the Nazi regime. But from a historical perspective, she won. In *The Diary of Anne Frank*, the Jewish teenager recorded a vivid account of the thoughts, the hopes, and the dreams of a young girl, hiding from Hitler's SS troops in Nazi-occupied Holland.

It's been said, "Victory has a thousand fathers, but defeat is an orphan." The inspiring stories of Luz Long and Anne Frank prove otherwise.

9

To lead a good life...

Fall down seven times, get up eight.

Refusing to seek honest advice, fools stay fools, sometimes forever. As if standing behind a pig eating cherries, they find themselves knee-deep in their own mistakes. Too proud to listen and too stubborn to change their ways, they race through life, wondering why they never cross the finish line ahead of the pack.

In contrast, those on a truer, more realistic path, approach their race differently. Void of ego and foolish pride, they crave, seek, and welcome honest advice. Accepting guidance and counsel, these genuine leaders have a better understanding of their strengths and weaknesses, more attuned to who they are and where they're going. Approaching their destination, their rewards are clearer, more intrinsic, and satisfying. In feeling a part of the process, those offering advice, share in their excitement, looking forward to the next challenge--the ultimate team-building experience.

In accepting the Image Award for Outstanding Actor, as only he can deliver, Denzel Washington offered his fellow actors the following advice:

> *"Without commitment, you'll never start. But more importantly, without consistency, you'll never finish. It's not easy. Keep working. Keep striving. Never give up. Fall down seven times, get up eight. Ease... is a greater threat to progress than hardship. (He repeats) Ease... is a greater threat to progress than hardship. So, keep moving, keep growing, keep learning. See you at work."*

Preaching from a lectern of experience, Denzel offered a group of aspiring young actors more of the same:

> *"You'll never see a U-Haul behind a hearse. Now I've been blessed to make hundreds of millions of dollars in my life, but I can't take it with me, and neither can you. It's not how much you have, it's what you do with what you have. And we all have different gifts. Some have money, some love, some patience, some the ability to touch other people, but we all have it. Use it. Share it. That's what counts. It's not what you're driving, flying in, not what kind of house you bought your momma. Dreams... without goals... are just dreams. And they ultimately fuel disappointment. Goals... on the road to achievement... cannot be achieved without discipline and consistency. I pray that you all put your shoes way under the bed at night, so you have to get on your knees in the morning to find them."*

With open arms, a willing heart, and honest intent, those on a mission to bridge the gap from good to great, put their egos aside, listen, reflect, sort, weigh, and balance words from the wise. Realizing, like an old loop film, the mind has a way of replaying failure and defeat, and because the pain of regret hurts so bad and runs so deep, they cherish solid guidance and reflective direction.

When all is said and done, however, as sure as the sun sets in the west, the best advice, over time, sinks and dwells upon a stark but challenging reality: All the advice in this world will never help until you help yourself. See you at work.

10

To lead a good life…

Break out the Hawaiian shirt and be inspired.

Dave and Janet Moore live in Port Clinton, Ohio. They were blessed with a daughter they truly loved. Jordan was a special-needs child, challenged with hearing loss, developmental delay, and autism. Dave and Janet completely dedicated themselves to giving her every opportunity to experience the joys of life. As she grew older, however, some opportunities became more challenging to provide.

Here's one example to help you understand their dedication. I'm quite certain it will lift and inspire you:

> On a calendar in her home, Jordan saw her parents were going to a wedding and with firm resolve, she said, "I want a wedding!" When they asked who she would like to marry, with a smile that would melt your heart, she exclaimed, "Daddy!"
>
> Realizing her life was slipping away, (due to declining kidneys) and since her 28th birthday was coming up, they decided to grant her wish and give her a wedding. They would call it, "A covenant of love between Jordan Elizabeth Moore and her family."
>
> Together, the family planned a full wedding and reception, complete with wedding dress, wedding rings-- provided by the family pastor--flowers, and music. Generous family friends would take care of the photography and another would make Jordan's wedding dress. As she was partially deaf, an interpreter would stand by the minister facing Jordan, making sure she

understood every word of the ceremony.

As planned, her entire family (mom, dad, brother, and sister) walked her down the aisle, poised, and ready to give Jordan the wedding day she deserved. The church was filled with over 150 friends, family, caregivers, and anyone else who made her life complete. The vows were fashioned from the book, Love You Forever, by Robert Munsch; "We'll love you forever, we'll like you for always, as long as we're living, our baby you'll be."

The reception theme was based on Jordan's favorite food, "Cheeseburgers in Paradise," complete with pineapples, sand, and beach toys on every table. In the spirit of the occasion, many a guest wore Hawaiian shirts. The cafeteria personnel from her hospital prepared the meals and her parents provided the cake. Daddy and Jordan danced the father-daughter dance to My Girl.

There are people in this world, like Dave and Janet Moore, living life to its fullest in the face of their everyday challenges, offering large doses of hope and inspiration. The next time you need a boost of creative genius, you might want to stop, take a deep breath, close your eyes, and picture the young lady with a huge wedding-day smile, walking down the aisle arm-in-arm with her family--the center of the room's attention--and loving every minute of it. If that doesn't give you a little boost, perhaps you're not ready to be inspired. Dave and Janet Moore, thanks for the lift.

Review: Stories 6 - 10

6

To lead a good life… tie the shoestrings and find your own inspiration.

You want inspiration--take a walk. That's it! Just put on your tennis shoes, open the front door, and start walking. As you go, make sure you stop, talk, and ask your neighbors a few questions about their life journeys and challenges. You may find enough inspiration to last a lifetime.

7

To lead a good life… find a way to get back home.

To thrive, to develop, to succeed, and to find happiness, we need support from home. It's the place we dream of getting back to when we find ourselves lost in a world of cold, hurt, or uncertainty.

8

To lead a good life… make all your victories of the soul and spirit.

Integrity is not kept by winning at all costs, but from within the parameters of your own values, thoughts, and actions. Like Luz Long, set aside personal gain and do what you believe to be right, just, and of the soul and spirit.

9

To lead a good life… fall down seven times, get up eight.

With open arms, a willing heart, and honest intent, those on a mission to bridge the gap from good to great, put their ego aside, listen, reflect, sort, weigh, and balance words from the wise. Realizing the mind, like an old loop film, has a way of replaying failure and defeat, they cherish solid guidance and reflective direction.

10

To lead a good life… break out the Hawaiian shirt and be inspired.

There are people in this world living life to its fullest in the face of their everyday challenges. The next time you need a boost of creative genius, stop, close your eyes, and picture the young lady with a huge wedding-day smile, walking down the aisle arm-in-arm with her family and loving every minute of it.

11

To lead a good life…

In tough times, play on the one string you have, your attitude.

Before we get too old and gray, if we're lucky, we'll figure out there are three things in life we can't change. Christian theologian and preacher Charles Swindoll, wrote, "We can't change our past, we can't change other people, and we can't change the inevitable. About all we can do is play on the one string we have, and that is our attitude." Healthy advice. Save a lot of headaches if some of us could've figured that out earlier in life, like this little guy:

> *One fall evening, about 8:00, the little guy knocked on the door. As though delivering a fresh bouquet, he greeted his neighbor with a broad smile.*
>
> *Wearing oversized jeans and a half-ironed, button-down shirt, his hair was slicked back and a tattered, old book back hung loosely over one shoulder.*
>
> *"What's going on? You look like you're ready for school?"*
>
> *"I am. My mom just got home. Sometimes she drinks too much. She thinks it's 8 in the morning." Fearing he would miss the bus, his mom panicked, scrambled to get him ready, and pushed him out the door.*
>
> *"Do you mind if I come in for a little while until she falls asleep. It usually doesn't take too long?"*
>
> *Leading him in, she asked, "Why didn't you tell her school was already over?"*

> *"I learned a long time ago, when she's been drinking, it's best to just shut my mouth and go with the flow."*
>
> *"Would you like something to eat?"*
>
> *"Yes, ma'am, I'm very hungry."*
>
> *Getting situated, like a child playing with a new puppy, he seemed upbeat, light-hearted, and carefree.*
>
> *After finishing his meal, he said, "I think it will be okay to go home now."*
>
> *He thanked her, grabbed his book bag, and pleaded, "Please don't think bad things about my mom. She has some problems, but she's a great mom, and she's my best friend."*

Somehow, in his unstable world, the youngster learned how to handle a tough home life. Realizing, as Swindoll prescribed, he couldn't change his mother's past or some of the poor decisions she's made in life, he decided to play on the one string he had... his attitude.

I've taught children who've battled the hurt of physical abuse, the strain of mental abuse, the emptiness of abandonment, and the pangs of poverty. At best, they get a school breakfast, a school lunch, and usually go home to little or no supper. Yet they manage to study, play the trumpet, dig a volleyball out of a net, cheer their team on, or participate in the school play. Their attitudes are good, they don't complain, and they aren't mad at the world. They get up every morning, give life all they've got, and try to make their lives complete. I'm not sure how they do it, but they do. Some of the best role models we have, as if defying their age, are those young people battling to see a better day. Sad but true.

12

To lead a good life...

Bathe in triumph, shower in accomplishment.

Bobby Knight, one of the most successful, demanding, and controversial college basketball coaches of his time, preached, "The mental is to the physical as four is to one."

What if the challenge pushed beyond the normal limits of what men and women are asked to endure? Would the ratio of mental to physical increase beyond four to one? I think Coach Knight would agree, in some instances, the challenges are so great and so traumatic, the ratio would be greater. Much, much greater:

> *All-day, every day, each step was a monumental challenge after a violent work accident left him with one leg, three toes, and a reconstructed knee. To walk, his focus in taking each step had to be near perfect, an intense demand of concentration during an uncommon challenge. With cane in hand, chin up, shoulders back, and a smile on his face, he met the challenge of each step, hefting that old, bulky, mannequin-like artificial limb, until he rested in peace, some twenty-two years after his accident.*
>
> *Though his walk was imperfect, part limp, part gallop, part strange, when he walked into a room, it was the smile you couldn't help but notice. By design, it was broad, mischievous, and clever, with intentions of diverting all focus, thought, and attention, not on the imperfection of his walk or the struggle in taking each step, but rather on the success and quiet celebration of each.*
>
> *Seeking no pity, no help, no sympathy or want, he sent*

> *a direct and powerful message for all to see. Bathed in*
> *triumph and showered in accomplishment, as if to say, "I*
> *can do this with pride and dignity," and he did. Oh yeah,*
> *and along the way, he helped raise eight children.*

Endurance swimmer Martin Strel knows something about mental and physical toughness. In 2007, he became the first man to swim the entire length of the Amazon River. Navigating dark and dingy waters, dangerous predators, tropical diseases, and hostile natives, he finished his 4,345-mile swim in 66 days.

Robert Peary understood uncommon triumph and accomplishment. He is credited with being the first man to reach the North Pole-‑considered to be the most difficult expedition on the planet. In 1909, despite the dangers of camping on thin ice, traveling over vast mounds of ice, the threat of frostbite, hypothermia, high winds, deadly polar bears, and the constant fear of falling into deep, unforgiving crevices, Peary and his crew finished their 304-mile expedition in 36 days and 22 hours.

Perhaps a million steps ago, my father, the man with one leg and three toes, started his ultramarathon. Knowing to succeed, each step, with firm intention and unwavering persistence, had to be of the same resolution as anyone swimming the Amazon River or walking to the North Pole.

With wooden cane in hand and that clever smile, he leveraged his stump and hefted his artificial limb, placing one foot firmly in front of the other, only to start the process over and over and over again. Not for 66 days or 36 days and 22 hours, but for the rest of his life, demanding the mental be to the physical, not as four is to one, but greater. Much, much greater.

13

To lead a good life...

Be like Myram.

Did you ever have a teacher who inspired you? What was it about them that made you work and gravitate toward them? I believe I know the answer. That teacher cared about you, saw something special in you, and worked from there.

Here's what I think: Teachers who inspire don't get blinded by a trendy curriculum, million-dollar technology, or long-distance field trips to the land of Oz. They focus on a simpler, less expensive, and less complicated approach. It's called empathy. It works. And it's free.

A teacher I worked with had the gift of empathy and used it to motivate her students:

> *I taught with Myram Ogden at Sts. Peter and Paul School in Sandusky, Ohio, back in the '70s. She truly cared about and found the best in both the teachers and the students she worked with. Through consistency of purpose and quiet respect, she was a leader in our school. God rest her soul, everybody loved Mi.*
>
> *A few days into my first year of teaching, I walked down the hall during my planning period. Taking note of the atmosphere in her room, I stopped, peered inside, and listened. I was captivated by her ability to control her class, how engaged her students were in the lesson, and the way they responded to her style of teaching.*
>
> *After school, I stopped by her room again and asked, "Mi, your discipline is so good and your students are so*

> *respectful and engaged, how do you create that atmosphere?"*
>
> *Her simple reply, "I teach."*
>
> *Confused, I asked, "Yeah, Mi, I know you teach, so do I, but how do you command that kind of respect?"*
>
> *"Listen closely... I teach. I get them so wrapped up in the subject matter and so engaged in what we're doing, they don't think about disrespecting. They know I enjoy the subject, they know I work hard to prepare, and they know I care. Look, do yourself a favor, prepare like crazy, show them you care, find the positive in each student, and work from there. The approach will work, and your students will love it."*

How lucky was I to get advice like that during my first year of teaching?

In 2018, Andria Zafirakou, a teacher from London, was nominated by her colleagues for the Varkey Foundation's annual Global Teacher Prize, dubbed "the Nobel for teaching." Those chosen would be judged on pupil progress, achievement outside the classroom, and their work in helping students become global citizens. There were 30,000 entries. Andria made the shortlist of nine finalists, flew to Dubai for the ceremony, and won the million-dollar first prize.

Like many of her fellow teachers, she worked with some of the most deprived, disadvantaged, and ethnically diverse children in her country. So, what made her the million-dollar educator? The short answer: She loved her work. She loved figuring out how to reach each child, how to get them to trust her, and how they could become better people.

In other words, like Mi Ogden, with empathy, she teaches. And so it is with leading and inspiring. Let people know you care, find the good in them, and work from there. It works, it's free, and both Myram Ogden and Andria Zafirakou, from opposite sides of the world, proved it.

14

To lead a good life…

Don't be afraid to sell your parrot to the town gossip.

With guidance, hopefully, we'll reach a point in our lives where we know what's right. We'll also reach a point in our lives, hopefully, where we know what's wrong. If we want to have a positive impact on those around us--and therein lies the challenge--we have to choose to do what's right… always. As American humorist Mark Twain of Huckleberry Finn notoriety, advised, "Lead your life so you wouldn't be ashamed to sell your parrot to the town gossip." Clever guy. Offered good advice.

There's been a beautiful story told in leadership circles over the years about doing things the right way. It originally appeared in *Chicken Soup for the Soul,* encouraging its readers to let integrity be their guide:

> *The nurse escorted the concerned Marine to a hospital bed.*
> *"Your son is here," she told the patient.*
> *As the old man was hard of hearing, she had to repeat herself before he smiled. To make him comfortable, the lights had been dimmed and he was now heavily sedated. The young Marine approached the bed, reached out, and wrapped his fingers firmly around the old man's hand, sending a quiet message of love, strength, and support.*
> *The nurse brought in a chair and the soldier settled in. Hours later, she suggested he get some rest and come back later. The Marine politely refused, staying bedside*

throughout the night.

At dawn, the old man quietly passed away. As the nurse tended to his lifeless body, she offered the soldier her sympathy. In mid-sentence, the tired Marine interrupted her and asked, "Who was that man?"

Startled by his question, she said, "Wasn't that your father?"

"No, he wasn't," replied the Marine. "I never saw him before in my life."

"Why didn't you say something when I brought you to his bed?"

As though receiving the Medal of Honor, he responded, "I knew there was a mistake, but I also knew he couldn't see me and he needed his son, so I stayed."

The compassionate soldier could've chosen a more convenient path, revealed who he was, and moved on. Letting integrity be his guide, with a heart of gold, he chose to sit down, wrap his fingers around the old man's hand, settle in, and do the right thing.

Like the bedside soldier, if you're going to lead, strive to make the right decisions… always. Then, without hesitation or concern, feel free to sell your parrot to the town gossip.

15

To lead a good life...

Keep your glass full at all times.

A wise man was asked, "When disappointed, do you see your glass half empty or half full?" With firm conviction, he said, "As I understand the value of staying positive, though sometimes hard to do, I keep my glass full at all times."

Vincent Van Gogh, one of the most famous and influential artists of all time, only sold one painting while he was alive. Just one. Refusing to be deterred, he didn't turn sour, blame the world, or quit chasing his dreams. He stayed positive and kept painting. Before he was done, he completed over 900 works of art.

Stephen King's first novel was rejected 30 times. Seeing his glass half empty, he gave up, threw his book into the trash, and walked away. His wife, refusing to be drawn into his negative reaction, retrieved the book, and encouraged him to keep trying. Today his books have sold over 350 million copies.

When Charlize Theron was 15, she witnessed her mother kill her father. Refusing to let the vision destroy her life, she stayed positive and went on to be the first South African actress to win an Academy Award.

Somewhere in my study of leadership, I came upon this simple and innocent lesson in staying optimistic:

> *A young girl and her father stopped at a roadside market to browse and buy some fresh fruits and vegetables. It was a beautiful fall day and both were*

happy just hanging out together. It was the kind of day a father and daughter remember for a lifetime.

Sitting on an old bench to rest and soak up the sun, the girl reached in one of the shopping bags and pulled out two perfectly shaped apples. Biting into one, she told her dad how juicy and delicious it was. When he asked if he could have the other, without hesitation, and to his surprise, she quickly bit into it. Instantly, he questioned her compassion and wondered where he'd gone wrong in teaching her about kindness and sharing.

Before his mind wandered too far into the negative, she turned to him saying, "Here, Dad, you take this one. I wanted to check which apple was the sweetest because I want you to have the best."

When the father reflects back on that beautiful fall day, I'm sure two thoughts cross his mind: First, he's happy he taught his daughter to be kind and considerate of others. Second, he's happy she taught him a valuable lesson about jumping to negative conclusions.

There are successful people all over this world, like Van Gogh, Mrs. King, and Charlize Theron, who strive to keep their glass full at all times. Though sometimes hard to do, they refuse to be denied. When their glass starts looking half empty, with a firm and steady pour, they quickly refill it. The next time you're challenged and get tired of pouring, just remember good old Vincent Van Gogh. He refilled his glass at least 899 times.

Picture this: I taught a young man who managed to see his glass half full. Some nights, he'd run to his bedroom and swing the door wide open. He'd crouch down behind it, grab the handle, pull the door close to his body, and hide between the door and the wall. Why? His dad would come home from the local bar and take his miserable existence out on his son. Yet the kid stayed positive in his quest to someday live a safer, more peaceful life. Today he's a successful businessman.

I also taught a brilliant young lady who stayed positive in the wake of disappointment. Her father refused to acknowledge her desire to earn a college degree. When she gathered enough nerve to sit down on the ottoman in front of his chair and discuss her intentions, he pulled his newspaper down to chest level, lowered his glasses toward the end of his nose, and listened to her plea. When she finished, without uttering a word or showing any emotion, he pushed his glasses back up tight to the bridge of his nose, raised the paper back up to eye level, and continued to read. Yet the girl stayed positive in her pursuit to someday further her education. Did she ever get her college degree? Sad to say the answer is no. She did, however, go to night school to get an associate's degree. As you'd guess, she never lost her positive attitude and is proud of what she's been able to accomplish.

Here's a bit of humble advice: The next time you come across a person who's staying positive while battling adversity, stop and let them know you're proud of them. Your words may help them fill their glass and give both of you a little boost of happiness. It sounds like a win-win situation to me.

11

To lead a good life... play on the one string you have, your attitude.

There are three things in life we can't change. In the words of preacher Charles Swindoll, "We can't change our past, we can't change other people, and we can't change the inevitable. About all we can do is play on the one string we have, and that is our attitude."

12

To lead a good life... bathe in triumph, shower in accomplishment.

Bobby Knight preached, "The mental is to the physical as four is to one." However, if your challenges push you beyond the normal limits of what men and women are asked to endure, the ratio would be greater. Much, much greater.

13

To lead a good life... be like Myram.

In leading and inspiring, let people know you care. With empathy, find the good in them and work from there. It works. And it's free.

14

To lead a good life... don't be afraid to sell your parrot to the town gossip.

Like the bedside soldier, if you're going to lead, strive to make the right decisions, letting integrity be your guide... always.

15 To lead a good life... keep your glass full at all times.

There are successful people all over this world who strive to stay positive at all times. Though sometimes hard to do, they refuse to be denied. When their glass starts looking half empty, they quickly refill it with positive thought and action.

16

To lead a good life...

Growl like The Strongman.

When you show strength and conviction, you never know who you might be inspiring. Without realizing it, you may be igniting a spark of hope inside those who witness your actions. Believing in yourself, driving yourself, and refusing to be denied enhances your chances of turning that spark into a flame that burns deep inside the belly of those who follow your lead.

Want proof? Sit back and enjoy the performance of... The Strongman:

> *The first-grader wheeled himself onto the stage. He'd been in a wheelchair most of his life, but on this day, he'd compete in the school talent show without his trusty wheels.*
>
> *Dressed like a superhero, complete with a bath towel tied around his neck and a big "S" sketched on the front of his t-shirt, he was ready to compete as... The Strongman. Crawling out of his chair, he scooted across the floor and grabbed a huge rubber ball by its handle. As his legs were hardened and lifeless, he struggled to mount the ball, but with the determination of a world-class mountain climber, he settled in.*
>
> *Using his stiff legs to secure stability and give direction, he started to bounce. Smiling at the audience, he proudly showed off his talents of balance, strength, and willpower. The more they cheered, the harder he bounced. Moving front and center, he stopped, and with a*

deep, tiger-like growl, he announced, "I am The Strongman."

As the cheering intensified, he bounced his way to the right side of the stage, stopped, adjusted his cape, and turned toward the audience. Growling louder, and with the confidence of a high-priced lawyer, he shouted over the wild applause, "I am The Strongman." With hands firmly clutching the handle, his head back, and his cape flapping, he bounced his way to the other side of the stage and did the same.

That's it. There was no song, no dance, no musical solo, just bouncing, stopping, growling, and ensuring the audience he was strong and confident.

Amid the standing ovation, and with a happiness he had never felt before, the young super-hero rolled off the rubber ball, crawled back to his trusty wheelchair, and confidently pushed himself off the stage.

The next time you find yourself challenged, like the young man in the talent show, hold tight, put a little bounce in your step, and give it all you've got. Though you may not garner a standing ovation for your efforts, with a growl and a radiant smile, you just might inspire those who follow your lead.

In hindsight, it seems kind of wild a first-grader managed to harness and release so much strength and conviction, but then again... he was The Strongman.

I worked with a child of similar strength and determination. Each morning it was common practice for our teachers to stand in the hall as students poured into the building. One young man caught my attention nearly every day. Though he had social, physical, and mental issues, each connected to abuse, he was a happy little guy.

I loved seeing him every morning because he was all dressed up, he was ready to go, and he was determined to have a good day. Through the trauma of all he had to deal with, he seemed cheerful and carefree. With his book bag over his shoulder, he high-stepped down the hall ready to take on the educational world.

By the end of the day, however, his problems, like a runaway train, seemed to catch and overtake him. The smile was gone, his clothes were disheveled, and that positive attitude turned to hateful sneers and violent outbursts. But as sure as hungry babies cry, the little guy would come the next morning with the same smile, the same positive attitude, and the same determination. Like The Strongman, he had a flame burning deep inside his belly to be successful, but he didn't have the physical or mental stamina to keep it lit throughout the day.

In witnessing his resilience, he lit a spark deep inside my belly, giving me the incentive to help other students slow their runaway train.

17

To lead a good life...

Adjust your sails.

Inspirational writer H. Jackson Brown, Jr., said, and sailors would agree, "When you can't change the direction of the wind, you adjust your sails." Staying positive in the throes of adversity requires the same thought and action.

A man who lived down the street from me when I was growing up, espoused the same beliefs, adjusting his sails every single day of his adult life. I wrote about him in a previous essay. My dad called him an American hero because he was. Truth be told, so was his wife:

> *He was drafted out of the halls of his high school and was wounded in the Hürtgen Forest in Germany during World War II. Remarkably, upon returning to the states, he spent the equivalent of three and a half years in a full-body cast. As he was wounded in the hip, for the rest of his life, each step was supported by a set of metal, Canadian crutches, and the faithful guidance of his wife.*
>
> *When asked if he was bitter about his plight, his response was firm and to the point, "Bitter? No, I'm not bitter. I'm proud of what I did for my country, and I'd do it again." Like my dad said, he was an American hero.*
>
> *When asked, "What was going through your mind, wounded, laying on the battlefield for over 24 hours, waiting for help?"*
>
> *His response painted a graphic picture of the realities of war, sending a haunting message that would stir the heart of any woman with sons or daughters fighting for*

> *their country in distant lands. As if recalling a never-ending nightmare, he said, "I remember being surrounded by hundreds of wounded soldiers, both enemy and ally, and the screams for help were horrible, each calling out for the same thing... 'Mommy!'"*

Though the young soldier couldn't change the direction of the shrapnel raining down from the treetops, when he returned home, he did adjust his sails. Refusing to turn negative and give up on life, he searched and found the right woman, one who would help him raise a family and navigate the winds of tough times. Day after day, he hefted those metal crutches and attacked life. Accepting the direction and guidance of his loving wife, he became a productive, successful, and respected citizen in the heart of the country he so readily defended.

Most military men and women espouse the same belief about finding the right partner. Because of the constant adjustments in the life of a soldier, it takes a strong, understanding, and patient spouse to marry a soldier.

How important is it to find the right person? Consider this: Known throughout the world as a master communicator, during World War II, Winston Churchill persuaded an entire nation to hunker down and stay strong as the German Luftwaffe dropped 30,000 tons of bombs on his country, killing 40,000 people.

By 1941 the German Blitzkrieg had failed and the British people, with the encouragement and guidance of Churchill, proved their toughness and resolve. Was that the Prime Minister's greatest accomplishment as a communicator? Not a chance. He believed his most brilliant achievement was his ability to persuade his wife to marry him.

A few years back, Ted Temper passed away. In true military fashion, he was buried just before Memorial Day weekend. Though we lost one American hero that day, we continued to witness another. When the American flag was removed from his casket and he was lowered into his grave, as she had done for so many years before, his wife stood by his side, making sure he rested in peace.

18

To lead a good life...

Use vibrant colors to paint your masterpiece.

Some said baseball immortal Babe Ruth was too undisciplined. Others felt basketball legend Michael Jordan was too skinny. Back in the day, the powers to be insisted baseball great Jackie Robinson was the wrong color. Founding Father Ben Franklin was a 10-year-old dropout, former President Andrew Jackson was an orphan, inventor Thomas Edison was an educational nightmare, and talk show host Oprah Winfrey was a fourteen-year-old, runaway mom.

The last I checked, each of the above reached world-class status in their respective professions. They recognized their challenges, used them as motivators, and refused to let circumstance alter their path to greatness.

So, what's holding you back? Is your boss too tough? You don't have the right last name? Or, maybe you come from the wrong side of the tracks? Here's a novel approach, go find someone who cares. Everybody's got their own problems. Like Jordan, the Babe, Ben Franklin, and the gang, you might as well just suck-it-up and move forward. I know, easy for me to say.

The next time you feel overwhelmed with your situation, you might want to think about a kid named Danny Bernard. Let me introduce you to him:

> *He was a good athlete, about 5'10" tall, strong legs and a solid build. He could stand under the basket, grab a volleyball, elevate, and slam dunk it through the hoop.*

When he played on the basketball courts behind the local junior high, the younger kids loved to watch him play against the taller guys. He inspired them, gave them hope--especially the short ones, uncertain they'd ever get a chance to play at the high school level.

During his senior year, he was in a terrible car accident and became a quadriplegic, spending the rest of his life--God rest his soul--confined to a wheelchair. With many of his hopes and dreams shattered, how did he respond? Did he turn negative, feel sorry for himself, and get mad at the world? Nope, not Danny Bernard--too much class for that. Though he never regained the use of his limbs, through hours and hours of extensive therapy, he became a painter. Let me relay that message to you again, he became a painter.

His nurse would dip the brush in the paint and place the handle in his mouth. Manipulating with his tongue, his teeth, and his lips, he painted by numbers. As you can imagine, the process was long, hard, and tedious.

Though paralyzed for life, there would be no dark, depressing colors in his pictures. He chose a more inspiring approach, using vibrant blends of reds, greens, and yellows. His pictures weren't of doomsday landscapes or apocalyptic night skies. Nope, he painted pictures of clown faces. Smiling faces. Happy faces. Danny Bernard was too positive to approach life any differently.

Visit the Louvre Museum in Paris, France, the Acropolis Museum in Athens, Greece, or the Metropolitan Museum of Art in New York City, and I have a feeling you won't find pictures more inspirational than Danny Bernard's, paint-by-number masterpieces.

So, the next time life splashes some heartache on your canvas, like Danny Bernard, just suck-it-up, grab a brush, and paint yourself a big, old colorful masterpiece. What's holding you back?

19

To lead a good life…

Treat the world as thine oyster and crack it open.

Ever hear the Shakespearean expression, "The world is thine oyster"? Good quote. In non-expert terms, it means: We have every advantage necessary to achieve what we wish to achieve… and enjoy life.

Good old William Shakespeare coined the phrase back in the day and finished his thought by writing, "Which I with sword will open." In other words, attack that oyster, crack it open, and get what you want out of life.

Regarded as the greatest writer in the history of the English language, he penned those words back in the 1500s, and they still resonate today. I guess that's why he's William Shakespeare.

There's an older gentleman, a very successful entrepreneur, who's in his late seventies. He seems to live by those words… and enjoys life:

> *Geno and his partner were on a short vacation in Florida, over eighteen hours from home. It was a beautiful day. He was swimming at the deep end of the pool, she was at the other end and didn't notice the sudden quiet. Eventually looking his way, she saw his ball-cap floating on the surface of the water; she didn't see him.*
>
> *When rescued, he had no vital signs. None. Working hard to resuscitate, miraculously, a few bystanders brought him back to life. Tough guy. Lucky guy.*
>
> *As he played cards on Monday nights with his high*

> *school buddies for over fifty years, he was bound and determined to get back home to continue the tradition. Not long after the traumatic experience, he was heading back, destined for another night of high-low poker.*
>
> *As the cards were being shuffled and dealt, it was obvious he was happy to be home, alive, and hanging out with the gang. Noticing his enthusiasm, one of the players said, "Hey, Geno, you've got a lot of energy tonight."*
>
> *With a sly, little smile and a touch of mischief in his eyes, he responded, "I oughta, I'm only about two weeks old!"*

Close to 80 years old and the mischief in his eyes has never dimmed. The smile, the sense of humor, the way he attacks life and what it has to offer, is a testament to his resilience and positive attitude. He's figured out, life is short and the old clock doesn't stop ticking too often. As there are few replays, rewinds, and do-overs, he knows, with sword in hand, you've got to grab that oyster, crack it open, achieve what you want... and enjoy life.

If the approach is good enough for Geno and Shakespeare, it oughta be good enough for you and me.

Make sense? Good. Now deal the cards.

20

To lead a good life…

On one leg or two, run toward the roar.

With stone-cold confidence, some people run toward the roar of adversity, priding themselves in making tough decisions. Others, at NASCAR speed, run away, hoping their problems, like smoke to wind, drift away.

Dwight D. Eisenhower knew something about making tough decisions. In the spring of 1944, as the Allied Supreme Commander in Europe, he had to make one of the most important decisions of World War II--exactly when and where to attack Europe.

As hundreds of thousands of troops, sailors, and airmen awaited his orders, he made sure his decision to storm the beaches of Normandy on June 6, reflected, not his fears, but rather the hopes and dreams of stopping the spread of Nazi tyranny. Because he was bold and confident, when he spoke, people listened.

A young man of similar strength had to make his own tough decision. Though his actions were not of global interest or world-wide consequence, on one good leg, he too ran toward the roar of adversity.

If you knew the kid and witnessed the way he attacked his decision, when he spoke, you'd listen to him, too:

> *In his early teens, Nick Lenyo was facing a major decision: have his lower leg removed, freeing him of cancer, or keep the leg, risking the spread of the deadly disease, more surgeries, and limited flexibility. As he also knew keeping the leg would dramatically reduce his chances of playing sports, and because he absolutely*

> *loved competition and being a part of a team, he made his decision: He'd have the lower part of his leg removed, relearn how to walk, and eventually compete with an artificial limb.*
>
> *After a full recovery, he was honored at a banquet in Cleveland for his courage. Introduced by Terry Francona, the manager of the Cleveland Indians, with a warm smile and the confidence of a world-class athlete, the teenager accepted the award and talked about his decision. The distinguished audience was mesmerized by his story and his positive outlook on life.*
>
> *In closing, balancing on his new, prosthetic leg, Nick looked at Jimmy Haslam, the owner of the Cleveland Browns, flashed a sly, little grin, and said, "Mr. Haslam, I understand you're looking for a quarterback. If you can wait a few more years, I'll be ready."*
>
> *The crowd loved it. Knowing his choice reflected, not his fears, but rather his hopes and dreams, they gave him a much deserved, standing ovation.*

The next time you're faced with making a tough decision, with the confidence of a general battling for his country, or a teenager learning to compete on one leg, run toward the roar of your adversity. Those around you will love it, be inspired by it, and when you speak, they'll listen to you, too.

21

To lead a good life…

Live the life you dreamed when you were young.

Imagine living the life you dreamed when you were young. If you did, do you suppose you'd be a different person today? Would you be happier, more confident, more secure? Do you think your life and the way you lived it would positively influence others? I'd bet big bucks it would. Guess what, it's never too late.

Here's a tragic, yet powerful passage about living life to its fullest and it's potential to positively influence others:

> *They were college girls, young, pretty, and vibrant, the kind who love life and everything it has to offer. Coming home from spring break, in an unforgiving heartbeat, a violent car accident took their lives, all six of them, ending their future hopes and dreams.*
>
> *When one of the mothers called and asked me to deliver her daughter's eulogy on campus, as the young girl's former elementary teacher, my reply was quick and from the heart, "It would be an honor." The journey to the podium, however, wasn't as easy.*
>
> *Driving to the college for the celebration of life was a challenge. The snowfall was relentless, the winds whipping the snow off the surrounding farmlands and onto the country roads made travel slow, tedious, and tiring. Like the snow, my thoughts drifted, thinking about the girls, their youth, enthusiasm, and potential, all shattered and lost, never to be returned.*
>
> *As the storm howled and the ice hardened, I wondered*

if the event would be canceled, robbing all involved of full closure. Knowing their classmates needed a chance to comfort and share their thoughts and prayers, I couldn't help but feel a bit empty. Against the force of the unforgiving winds, I shouldered the door open, put my head down, leaned forward, and headed towards the basketball arena.

The scene inside stunned my senses. The gymnasium, capable of holding thousands, was packed. Like marble statues, the students sat in total silence, each composed, ready to pay homage to their fellow students. Determined to pay their respects, they traipsed across campus, bundled in heavy jackets, winter boots, and thick gloves. Their solitude and presence reflected the trauma of the accident and just how vibrant and beautiful these young ladies' lives had been.

Although each eulogy was eloquent and heartfelt, the number of people, their attentiveness, and their resolve in braving the elements were more powerful than any words spoken that evening. Those six young ladies, in the process of living life to its fullest, positively influenced an arena full of people proving, as Abe Lincoln once said, "It's not the years in a life, it's the life in the years."

22

To lead a good life…

Have the courage to lose sight of the shore.

Every day we have a choice to make. As though preparing to win a national title, we can hop up out of bed with a smile on our face, challenge ourselves, and get started. Or, as though preparing to create nothing more than another losing season, we can stay in bed, pull the covers up over our head, and delay the process. Like I said, it's our choice.

Before we pull the covers up, stay in bed, and eventually make fools of ourselves, I think we'd be well served to follow the lead of a young lady on a mission to get a simple drink of water:

> *Each morning, at exactly the same time, the teacher took his fourth-grade class for a drink and a restroom break. If you've spent any time in an elementary school classroom, you understand the need to stay on a strict schedule. Routine is vital in providing any semblance of order and peace throughout the day.*
>
> *Early in the year, as they traveled down the hall, the teacher noticed a special-needs student and her aide coming down the hall from the opposite direction. Struggling hard, the young lady had trouble moving her legs in rhythm with the rest of her body. As she maneuvered toward the drinking fountain with the help of her crutches, she always had a smile on her face, but it didn't mask her determination to keep a steady pace.*
>
> *At first, she'd arrive at the drinking fountain about the time the teacher's class was finishing up and heading*

> *back down to their classroom. As the year progressed, however, she improved her pace and was reaching her destination earlier and earlier. In fact, on one of the last days of school, they were approaching the drinking fountain at the same time.*
>
> *Getting closer, the young lady picked up her pace and her smile broadened. A few feet away, she kicked it into another gear and lunged toward the fountain. Pushing one crutch aside, she caught the handle just before one of his students did. Arching her back, she looked up, smiled, and said, "I finally beat you guys!"*
>
> *It was a race! All year long she was competing against the class, each day challenging herself to move a little faster.*

Author William Faulkner once wrote, "You cannot swim for new horizons until you have the courage to lose sight of the shore." With a smile on her face, the young lady racing down the hall wasn't afraid to make her own choices, challenge herself, and lose sight of the shore.

Every day, as if pursuing hockey's Stanley Cup, she hustled down the hall, determined to win her self-imposed marathon. Finally, on one of the last days of the school year, she lunged, pushed that crutch aside, and reached her new horizon--the handle of the drinking fountain.

Review: Stories 16 - 22

16
To lead a good life... growl like The Strongman.
When you show strength and conviction, you never know who you might be inspiring. Without realizing it, you may be igniting a spark of hope inside those who witness your actions.

17
To lead a good life... adjust your sails.
Sailors understand when you can't change the direction of the wind, you change focus and direction. Staying positive in the throes of adversity requires the same thought and action.

18
To lead a good life... use vibrant colors to paint your masterpiece.
Recognize your challenges, use them as motivators, and refuse to let circumstance alter your path to greatness. Go ahead. What's holding you back?

19
To lead a good life... treat the world as thine oyster and crack it open.
Life is short and the old clock doesn't stop ticking too often. As there are few replays, rewinds, and do-overs, with sword in hand, you've got to grab that oyster, crack it open, achieve what you want... and enjoy life.

20
To lead a good life... on one leg or two, run toward the roar.
The next time you're faced with making a tough decision, with the confidence of a general battling for his country, or a teenager learning to compete on one leg, get up in the face of your adversity. Those around you will love it, be inspired by it, and when you speak, they'll listen.

21

To lead a good life... live the life you dreamed when you were young.

It's time. Your time. Refresh, rekindle, start over. Live the life you envisioned when you were young and get back to positively influencing others. It's never too late.

22

To lead a good life... have the courage to lose sight of the shore.

Every day we have a choice to make. We can hop up out of bed, challenge ourselves, and strive to reach our potential. Or, as though preparing to create nothing more than another losing season, we can stay in bed, pull the covers up over our head, and delay the process. It's our choice.

Part 2

Leadership

"Power creates distance. Leaders close the gap."
Texas Secretary of State Phil Wilson

"The most powerful leadership tool you have is your
own example."
College Basketball Coach John Wooden

"No great genius has ever existed without a touch of madness."
Greek Philosopher Aristotle

"Not the cry, but the flight of a wild duck leads the
flock to fly and follow."
Chinese Proverb

"Leadership development is self-development."
Management Consultant John G. Agno

"Leaders don't create followers; they create more leaders."
Anonymous

"The leader is the one who, out of the clutter,
brings simplicity... out of discord, harmony... and
out of difficulty, opportunity."
Theoretical Physicist Albert Einstein

23

To lead a good life...

Introduce yourself to the cleaning lady.

Talk to any group of accomplished leaders, and here's something most will agree upon: Few skills in the life of a leader are more valuable than networking. Connecting with others broadens their base of support and opens infinite doors of opportunity--a necessary step in reaching one's maximum potential. A wise leader, one destined to reach the highest levels of success, leaves no stone unturned in bringing good people, young and old and from all walks of life, into his or her world.

Do you want real success? Get in your shiny new Maserati, or your rusty old jalopy, ride off into the sunset and start networking. With clear intentions of developing meaningful relationships, share your ideas, feed off of their ideas, and develop a positive and friendly rapport with each. Then, jump back into that $135,000 luxury vehicle of yours, or that clunker you bought for 500 bucks, and continue your journey.

Like a starving hunter, track successful people down. Like a desperate farmer, cultivate each relationship. And like a shrewd entrepreneur, market yourself, your uniqueness, what you have to offer, and what you stand for. Then, put that auto back in high-gear and keep driving, determined to build a foundation of friendship, support, and understanding. As networking is a lifelong quest, you'll put more and more miles on that vehicle, but the journey will be worth the time and effort.

In an article entitled *"Know the Cleaning Lady: A Lesson in People,"* award-winning author Amy Taylor, shares the following lesson on networking:

> *It was the young man's first semester of college. Being a proud business student, he meticulously prepared himself for every class. At mid-semester, he was greeted in one of his classes with a pop quiz. Because he had breezed his way through all previous tests and quizzes, he was confident, on this day, he would do the same. And he did. Until the last question. It read: "What is the first name of the woman who cleans this classroom?"*
>
> *Though he saw the woman every morning he had class and knew she worked hard to keep the building clean, he had never taken the time to introduce himself. Regrettably, he left the last answer blank. Before leaving, one of the students asked the professor if the last question counted for a grade.*
>
> *With firm resolve, he responded, "Absolutely! In your careers, you will meet many people. All are significant. They each deserve an introduction. It takes a minute, shows you care, and puts some meaning behind a smile, a nod, or a simple hello."*

To win the game, you must remain in the game, and an all-encompassing approach to networking enhances those chances. As business magnate Steve Jobs reminded, "Great things in business are never done by one person. They're done by a team. Build wisely and with open arms." And be sure to introduce yourself to the cleaning lady.

24

To lead a good life...

Develop a heart that gives.

A common thread weaves deeply into the fiber of greatness, giving credence to this universal thought: To fully develop the leader within, you must practice and master the selfless art of giving.

To those who follow, a leader must give endless time, energy, enthusiasm, and expertise. It's a yeoman's task, but when done correctly, those actions inspire others to climb higher, dig deeper, accomplish more, and become more. If the gift of giving can be sustained over a long period, the almighty summit of leadership will be reached and kept.

Did you ever wonder who inspired a resilient leader like Nelson Mandela? Who influenced a talented novelist like Pearl S. Buck, a creative musician like John Lennon, a mathematical genius like Albert Einstein, or a legendary businessman like Steve Jobs? Who has that kind of impact? Who reaches that level of influence?

Here's a revelation: Mandela, Buck, Einstein, Lennon, and Jobs, gave credit to Indian leader Mahatma Gandhi as a source of their inspiration. Gandhi's willingness to give of himself, like a seasoned blacksmith, drove rivets of strength and endurance deep into his legacy as a leader, inspiring men and women around the world to do the same.

Gandhi, the man who said, "The best way to find yourself is to lose yourself in the service of others," reached and surpassed that almighty summit of leadership. Verifying Gandhi's global influence, Nobel-prize-winning playwright George Bernard Shaw, said, "Impressions of

Gandhi? You might well ask someone's impressions of the Himalayas." That's high praise.

Dan Millman, in "*Chicken Soup for the Soul 20th Anniversary Edition*," wrote an inspirational piece about a young boy's willingness to make the ultimate sacrifice of giving:

> *His sister was suffering from the same disease he survived and now she needed blood. As luck would have it, her younger brother had developed the antibodies that would combat her illness.*
>
> *When the doctors approached the five-year-old boy and explained the situation, without hesitation he replied, "Yes, I'll do it if it will save Liza."*
>
> *Being young, he didn't fully understand what he was asked to do. As he lay next to his sister for the transfusion, he looked over at her, smiled, and said, "Will I start to die right away."*

Though the little guy may never be mentioned in the same breath with influencers like Mandela, Einstein, Buck, Lennon, Jobs, or Gandhi, his selflessness and courage deserve high praise. At age 5, he'd already driven a few powerful rivets deep into his legacy as a leader.

In the classic Chinese text, referred to as the *Tao Te Ching*, it is written, "The heart that gives, gathers." If a person wants to inspire others to reach unparalleled levels of success, they'd be wise to follow the lead of the little boy, develop a heart that gives, and start gathering.

25

To lead a good life…

Trust everybody, but cut the deck.

A fire brigade rushed to the scene of a burning building to save a young man standing on a ledge ten-stories up. The firemen shouted, "Jump, and we'll catch you in the blanket."

The young man shouted back, "I don't trust you guys. Lay the blanket on the sidewalk and I'll jump."

An experienced leader offered three thoughts on trust. "First, like any solid foundation, it takes time to build. Second, it takes but a heartbeat to destroy, often leaving nothing more than broken promises and unfulfilled dreams. And third, trust has some of the same qualities as a rose; once a pedal has fallen, it'll never be perfect again."

There is an old newspaper story about trust that has been told over and over again. And though its source has never been verified, its message is solid:

> *He woke, walked to the bedroom window, peered through the blinds to check the weather, and was shocked to see his car was gone. Calling the police, they assured him they'd do everything in their power to find it.*
>
> *Three days later, he woke, walked to the window, peered through the blinds to check the weather, and noticed his car was back in the driveway as if it were never stolen.*
>
> *Opening the door of the vehicle, he found a dozen, long-stem roses, and a handwritten note: "I'm sorry I took your car. I had a family emergency and desperately*

needed a vehicle. I promise I'll never take from you again."

The note was not signed, but next to the flowers was a pair of tickets to a local concert. That weekend, he took his wife out to eat, went to the concert, and had a wonderful time.

Arriving home, he was shocked to find his house had been cleaned out--completely.

Like a cold slap in the face, the man with the concert tickets and a handful of long-stem roses experienced the realities of trust. He found out the hard way, it must be built on consistency of purpose over a long period of time. It must be earned, not through words or gifts or promises, but rather through consistent deed and action. And finally, once trust has been broken, like that rose without a pedal, it'll never be perfect again.

Confucius, a philosopher born in 551 and still quoted today, once remarked, "Rulers need three resources: weapons, food, and trust. The ruler who cannot have all three should give up weapons first, then food, but should hold on to trust at all costs. Without trust, we cannot stand."

The next time you're challenged with issues of trust, standing on the ledge of a burning building, or playing poker with your last dime, before you make a leap of faith, you'd be wise to follow the clever advice of American humorist and writer Finley Peter Dunne, who wrote, "Trust everybody, but cut the deck."

26

To lead a good life...

Stay disciplined... rain or shine.

The military prepares, not for games played on local, artificial turf, hardwood floors, or perfectly manicured golf courses, but rather for life and death situations on high-stake battlefields throughout the world. They realize their chances of success are predicated on a no-nonsense, in-your-face type of discipline, used to reach unthinkable levels of perseverance. As General George Washington stated, "Discipline is the soul of an army. It makes small numbers formidable; procures success to the weak, and esteem to all."

In *Developing the Leader Within You*, John C. Maxwell shares the following story:

> *A sergeant was in charge of keeping the grass green in front of the administrative building. He ordered a private to water the area every day at exactly five o'clock.*
>
> *During a terrible storm, the sergeant came into the barracks at five and found the private in a deep sleep.*
>
> *"What's the matter with you? Why aren't you watering the grass!"*
>
> *"It's raining, sir."*
>
> *"You've got a raincoat, haven't you?"*

The common man sees foolishness in the sergeant's orders. Experienced leaders, especially those hardened by the realities of war, completely understand his approach. For success to be reached and maintained in any endeavor, big or small, team or individual, discipline cannot be a part-time commitment. Though it doesn't have to be of military harshness, it has to be constant, consistent, and complete.

Consider three of Michelangelo's artistic accomplishments: Without discipline, there'd be no awe-inspiring Pieta, chiseled from a single slab of marble, depicting Mother Mary cradling her crucified son. Without discipline, there'd be no flawless statue of David, reproducing the beautiful symmetry of man's body, combining youthful beauty, grace, and strength. Without discipline, there'd be no breathtaking paintings on the barrel-vaulted ceiling of the Sistine Chapel, depicting stories from the Old Testament.

How much time, effort, and discipline did Michelangelo put into his work? In his own words, he said, "If people knew how hard I worked to get my mastery, it wouldn't seem wonderful at all."

Through experience, skilled leaders realize discipline is the great connector of goals to accomplishment. Without it, there's little chance of consistent results. With a clear purpose and noble intent, not as a tool of punishment, retaliation, or humiliation, it's a leader's responsibility to find the appropriate levels and methods of discipline and start connecting... rain or shine.

27

To lead a good life...

Avoid being a fool on a hill.

Leadership author John Maxwell, once said, "He who thinks he leads but has no followers, is only taking a walk." Most leaders agree, to ensure a following, three challenges must be addressed:

- First, like an ironworker bending rebar, work hard to master all strengths.

- Second, without deception or pretense, acknowledge all weaknesses.

- Third, as if preparing for a college entrance exam, develop a consistent and reasonable plan to accomplish both.

If you can't master all three, when charged to lead, you'll find yourself, like a fool on a hill, taking long, lonely walks.

In the book *Every-day Life of Abraham Lincoln*, American author Francis Fisher Brown shared the following insight into Lincoln's military, leadership skills--or the lack thereof:

> *Lincoln put together a volunteer company to fight in the Black Hawk War. As he brought the group together, he assumed leadership of his men and was given the rank of captain. There was, however, one major problem: having no experience, Lincoln knew nothing about*

> *soldiering or tactics. In fact, he had trouble remembering the simplest military instructions.*
>
> *For example, one day, as he was marching his men from one field to another, he came upon a narrow gate separating the two. As he couldn't remember the commands to put them into a tighter formation, he shouted, "This company is dismissed for two minutes, when it will fall in again on the other side of the gate."*

Lincoln never mastered the art of soldiering. He finished his military career as a private. He was, however, smart enough to be honest with himself about his leadership skills and limitations. Steering away from soldiering, he found a calling more suited to his talents. He ended up leading, not a company of men, but rather a nation, lost in the bloodshed of its own, horrific Civil War.

From private to Commander in Chief, there would be no fool on a hill for Abe Lincoln. Without pause, he recognized, acknowledged, outsourced, and even appreciated his leadership flaws. Working hard to master all strengths and address all weaknesses, he surrounded himself with people who complimented his skills. With remarkable resilience and steadfast influence, they worked together, leading their country out of the depths of its own, unforgiving hell.

Three legendary, Hall of Fame college coaches were specific in their philosophies on admitting mistakes. Duke basketball coach Mike Krzyzewski preaches, "When a leader makes a mistake and doesn't admit it, he is seen as arrogant and untrustworthy. And 'untrustworthy' is the last thing a leader wants to be."

Former Alabama football coach Bear Bryant agreed, saying, "When you make a mistake, there are only three things you should ever do about it: admit it, learn from it, and don't repeat it."

And former UCLA basketball coach John Wooden, once wrote, "You can make mistakes but you aren't a failure until you start blaming others for those mistakes."

When Krzyzewski, Bryant, or Wooden walked into a room to talk leadership, other coaches flocked to hear them speak. As with Lincoln, there would be no fool on a hill when they presented themselves and their philosophies on leadership. They worked hard to master their craft, acknowledged their deficiencies, and developed a reasonable plan to carry out both.

23
To lead a good life... introduce yourself to the cleaning lady.

Like a starving hunter, track successful people down. Like a desperate farmer, cultivate each relationship. And like a shrewd entrepreneur, market yourself, your uniqueness, what you have to offer, and what you stand for. It's the trademark of greatness.

24
To lead a good life... develop a heart that gives.

As a leader, you must give of yourself and your talents often, for the rewards of servitude are plenty.

25
To lead a good life... trust everybody, but cut the deck.

There are three virtues that need to be understood about trust. "First, it takes time to build. Second, it takes but a heartbeat to destroy, and third, trust has some of the same qualities as a rose. Once a pedal has fallen, it'll never be perfect again."

26
To lead a good life... stay disciplined... rain or shine.

Skilled leaders realize discipline is the great connector of goals to accomplishment. It's a leader's responsibility to find the appropriate levels and methods of discipline and start connecting.

27
To lead a good life... avoid being a fool on a hill.

There's an old proverb that states, "He who thinks he leads but has no followers, is only taking a walk." To ensure a following, work hard to master all strengths, acknowledge all weaknesses, and develop a consistent and reasonable plan to accomplish both.

28

To lead a good life…

Look to the heavens wearing work boots.

When questioned about their ability to impact and influence others, proven leaders offer no magic wands, potions, or tea leaves. Their suggestions are grounded in reality, offering nothing strange, peculiar, or bizarre. They'll propose a simple, straight-forward approach, assuring success is nothing more than a reflection of hard work and honest effort. That's it.

As if tired of suggestions otherwise, they'll stress forgetting about smoke and mirrors, sleight-of-hand, or pulling rabbits out of a hat. They'll assure you it's okay to hit your knees and look to the heavens for help, but when you put your hands together to pray you better have a little dirt under your fingernails and some mud on your boots.

The lady in the story below, whose author is unnamed, seems to have that hard work and honest effort thing all figured out:

> *A woman was busy working in her garden when a traveling minister rode by in his carriage. He stopped and said, "Young lady, what a wonderful garden you have. It's beyond beautiful."*
>
> *The garden was in full bloom. It was bordered with vibrant roses and flourishing lilies. Each row was picture perfect, completing the most magnificent garden he had ever seen.*
>
> *The woman stopped and looked up at him as he continued, "My good woman, God certainly has blessed you with this extraordinary garden."*

> *Standing up, she brushed the rich soil from her knees, wiped the sweat from her brow, and replied, "Yes, I am blessed, but you should have seen this garden when He had it all to himself."*
>
> *As the minister rode away, he took note of all the other gardens in the neighborhood. Each had the same soil, the same amounts of sunlight, and the same opportunity for growth, but none as pleasing as hers. At that moment he smiled, understanding each garden was nothing more than a reflection of the gardener's hard work and honest effort.*

To attain "beyond beautiful" results, there are three early-morning habits I believe hard-working influencers would agree upon:

- One, wake up, wipe the sleep from your eyes, and get ready to take on the world.

- Two, as there is no elevator to success, leap out of bed, strap on the work boots, and diligently climb the stairs.

- Three, understand million-dollar dreams become nothing more than fool's gold with a 25-cent work ethic.

Johannes Gutenberg didn't hope to pull a rabbit out of a hat when he changed the way we store and share knowledge and literature. Believing hard work betrays no one, he invented the movable-type printing press in the 15th century.

In the face of intense social pressure, Elizabeth Blackwell didn't use smoke and mirrors when she became the first woman in America to graduate from medical school. She decided to try a more logical approach. Investing in nothing more than a high-dollar work ethic, she finished first in her class.

And Austrian composer Wolfgang Amadeus Mozart didn't become one of the greatest composers in the history of Western music practicing sleight-of-hand, preparing magic formulas, or reading tea leaves. Instead, he invested in a lifetime of intense training. Although he was born with a gift, he insisted, "One is completely mistaken if they believe my art came to me with ease. I can assure you, good friend, no one put more effort into the study of composition than I have."

At the end of the day, if you've given it your best shot, when you put your head on your pillow late at night you'll be assured of a deeper, more satisfying sleep. Continuous hard work and honest effort--with a little mud on the boots and dirt under the fingernails--promises positive impact and lasting influence. That simple, unremarkable approach, also calms restlessness, diminishes anxiety, and offers a more fulfilling time to sleep, to dream, to wake, and to strap on the work boots, looking to the heavens with a smile on your face, ready to take on the world.

29

To lead a good life…

Provide a single thread of hope.

Confidence is an important stepping stone on the path to success. Once developed, it makes life easier, more productive, and much more rewarding. As it is with all skills, however, once confidence has been lost, the path quickly becomes a stepping stone to fear, doubt, frustration, and quit.

Writer Cloris Kylie lost her confidence early in life. After receiving the news that she wouldn't be accepted into the college of her choice, she found herself second-guessing her every move. Refusing to be defeated, she worked harder, studied more, and accomplished more. Taking small but deliberate steps, she methodically regained her confidence and went on to become a #1 best-selling author.

American soldier and politician Ulysses S. Grant lost faith in himself a number of times. Accused of drinking on duty, the West Point graduate left the Army, struggled financially, and was barely able to support his family. By the time the Civil War was over, he had become the top U.S. general and went on to become the 18th president of the United States.

Like Kylie and Grant, writer and humorist Mark Twain lost his competitive edge. Making bad business decisions, he lost his money and declared bankruptcy. Rising up out of the ashes of his early mistakes, he went on to become one of America's most loved and renowned authors.

To help someone regain confidence, you must find a way to take that person back to the exact moment it was lost, set a methodical plan of attack, and diligently start over. Though humbling, it's an honest process, involving intense perseverance and unlimited patience.

As in the passage below, when confidence is rebuilt and developed, it offers a lifetime of rewards worth pursuing for all involved:

> *The teacher sat the eighth-grader down to tutor him in reading. He was a big, strong, tough kid, sporting a colorful mohawk and crude tattoos on his forearms. As is the case with most troubled students, he had an edge to him.*
>
> *As he was reading at just a third-grade level, he was relieved to get out of the regular classroom, far away from the fear of being singled out and humiliated. Almost every day of his educational life, he sat in the back of the room, head down, fearing he would be called on to read in front of his peers. The chip on his shoulder was nothing more than a smoke-screen, diverting attention from embarrassment and the humiliating realities of failure.*
>
> *Understanding the process was going to be long and humbling, the tutor was understanding, yet brutally honest with the young man about the challenges they faced. With skill, passion, and persistence, the teacher convinced the young man he cared and quickly gained his trust. Together, as a team of two, they began the process at a level he could experience success--a third-grade level. A tough reality check, but a necessary one.*
>
> *The stories were simple and short, but the young man could read them, and he did pretty good answering the comprehension questions at the end of each story. On about the third day, it started to happen. He got all the answers correct, and the teacher put an A at the top of his paper. When he handed it to the young man, he stared at it for a moment, took a deep breath, and whispered, "Thank you. I never got an A before." And the process kicked into another gear.*

Being honest with himself, the student agreed to go back to the exact moment his confidence was lost, accept a structured plan of attack, and diligently started over. Though it was a tedious process, the young student, the tough guy--complete with tattoos, a mohawk, and a bit of an edge--reached new levels of confidence.

With a single thread of hope involving intense perseverance and unlimited patience, teacher and student together, carved a new path, offering a lifetime of rewards worth pursuing. For the teacher, it was a chance to change a life. For the student, it was the realization he was worthy and capable of reaching his dreams--a couple of paths worth pursuing.

30

To lead a good life...

Put a little burst of sunshine in someone's day.

Treasure and savor the gift from within your heart called kindness. It holds tightly to the keys to your success. Taking that thought to a deeper, more personal level, offering kindness during another person's despair has the potential to prepare and lift both to greatness.

An unknown author once wrote, "A little spark of kindness can put a colossal burst of sunshine into someone's day." It's one of those gifts everyone can afford, everyone likes to receive, and without much effort, it enriches meaningful relationships.

A leader of vision, as though panning gold, searches opportunities to extend a little thoughtfulness to individuals from within his or her team and builds from there:

> *The new supervisor walked the floor of the plant and introduced himself to one of his workers. In conversation, the employee mentioned his excitement about watching his son play in his first varsity football game that night at the local high school. The new boss smiled and encouraged him to enjoy every minute of his son's season.*
>
> *They shook hands and parted ways. Because the new supervisor had taken a few minutes out of his day to introduce himself and ask about family, the worker went about his day with a little extra burst of energy.*
>
> *Arriving at the game early, the proud father stopped at the concession stand, bought a box of popcorn, a candy bar, and something to drink. Moving to his seat on the*

fifty-yard line, trying to balance all he had bought, he didn't notice the man moving in behind him. When he turned to look, he was shocked to see his new boss sitting down next to him.

Smiling from ear-to-ear, his boss said, "I love high school football. I thought I'd come and share in your excitement."

The new supervisor's simple act of kindness, resulting in a little burst of sunshine, didn't cost much, didn't take long to execute, and was of little effort. And though he connected with only one of his workers that night, he connected with one. The perfect start in the development of team--a solid team, one primed and ready to work together as one.

People of lasting impact have their own thoughts and beliefs on kindness. Adored by millions, Princess Diana of Wales encouraged her followers to be kind, saying, "Carry out a random act of kindness, with no expectation of reward, safe in the knowledge that one day someone might do the same."

Amelia Earhart, who captured the world's imagination as a pioneer in flight, put her own spin on kindness, saying, "A single act of kindness throws out roots in all directions, and roots spring up new trees."

And American-British novelist Henry James, considered by many to be one of the greatest novelists in the English language, had a few thoughts on kindness, writing, "Three things in human life are important. The first is to be kind. The second is to be kind. And the third is to be kind."

Princess Diana, Amelia Earhart, Henry James, and the new supervisor realized the value and rewards of kindness. As Plato, the founder of the first institution of higher learning, once wrote, "Kindness is more than deeds. It's an attitude, an expression, a look, a touch. It is anything that lifts a person."

Go ahead, kindness is free. Like pollen in the wind, spread it everywhere, and enjoy the burst of sunshine.

31

To lead a good life…

Grab a chair, any chair, and sit down.

Fear-based leaders are usually one-trick-ponies. They spend their time fueling their needs with threats, intimidation and scare tactics. That's it. And it works… for a while. But before long the fuse of dysfunction has been lit, the flames gather speed, and all teamwork self-implodes.

Gifted leaders develop and maintain success with a blend of empowerment, inspiration, and cooperation. They believe elevating others broadens their base of influence and heightens their cause. They also realize fear stifles creativity and strangles cooperation, eventually turning the team away from the goal. Worry and survival become the driving force behind collaborative thoughts and actions, ultimately silencing transparency, choking innovation, and breeding negative behavior.

Void of open and honest dialogue, authenticity, and collaboration, like plants without water, eventually wither and die. Before long, those caught in the clutches of fear-based leaders understand the approach is nothing more than a mask to conceal insecurities, hide ineptitude, and disguise poor leadership skills--and the implosion continues.

When the owner of a successful vegetable business quietly walked into his own conference room, he sent a different leadership message altogether:

> *Farmer Jones, the owner of Chef's Garden, a globally successful business in Milan, Ohio, quickly blended in.*

Having no desire to stand out, he asked no glorious entrance, no pompous introduction, or self-centered fanfare. Realizing meaningful leadership focuses on the team, he had no need to bask in any pretentious, self-serving limelight.

A man of experience, navigating his company through the good times and the bad, he knows how to motivate his workforce. He's learned, to succeed in any business, you must empower your team and create an atmosphere of ownership, making sure each cog in the wheel tastes the sweetness of victory and shares in the bitterness of defeat.

When the meeting was called to order, Farmer Jones didn't sit at the head of the conference table. His choice was as low-keyed as his entry. He just grabbed a chair, one exactly like everyone else's, and sat down.

The meeting was void of wielding power, status, or authority. It was a sharing session, encouraging both give and take from everyone in the room. There was a lot of listening and plenty of respect. When a question came up, the first words out of his mouth were telling: "Well... what do you guys think?" And the give and take and quiet respect continued.

When called to lead, ask yourself these two questions:

- First, are you a one-trick, fear-based pony? If the answer is yes, don't unpack your bags, you won't be in charge long.

- Second, is your team front and center or is it all about you? If the limelight shines only on you, bask in the glow now, because before you know it, you'll be riding off into the sunset on your one-trick pony, wondering what could've been.

Like Farmer Jones, political leader Nelson Mandela didn't believe the limelight should shine only on himself. He believed, "It is better to lead from behind and put others in front, especially when you celebrate victory when nice things occur. You take the front line when there is danger. Then people will appreciate your leadership."

Leadership author and speaker John C. Maxwell doesn't believe a person of influence should be a one-trick, fear-based leader. He believes, "The single biggest way to impact an organization is to focus on leadership development. There is almost no limit to the potential of an organization that recruits good people, raises them up as leaders, and continually develops them."

American author and successful entrepreneur Seth Godin doesn't believe in silencing transparency or stifling creativity, saying, "Leadership is the art of giving people a platform for spreading ideas that work."

Whether you're fighting for equality in South Africa with Mandela, teaching leadership throughout America with Maxwell, writing books with Grogin at his home in New York, or planting vegetables for Chef's Garden with Farmer Jones in Ohio, leading, inspiring, and motivating others is all the same. Forget about the limelight, ruling with an iron fist, or masking insecurities. Just grab a chair, any chair, sit down and be humble, genuine, and honest. Then unpack your bags and stay awhile.

32

To lead a good life...

Downshift and turn the corner.

There's been a tall tale told over the years about the challenges of leading a diverse group of individuals. The narrative goes something like this:

> *On the first day of school, the first third grader in the door was in a three-piece suit. His hair was slicked back and neatly parted, his shoes were spit-shined, and his burgundy socks matched his vest. As if owning the place, he walked into the room with authority, carrying a briefcase in one hand and a newly sharpened, No. 2 pencil in the other. Stopping by the teacher's desk, he introduced himself, placed his trusty pencil behind his ear, and shook the teacher's hand. In military fashion, he turned and promptly found his desk. Opening his briefcase, he proceeded to pull out two books: The Rise and Fall of the Third Reich and Saint Augustine's Confessions.*
>
> *The teacher's thoughts, "This is going to be a great year!"*
>
> *The second student in the classroom was different-- much different. He scooted in the door, pretending to drive a race car. With arms extended, as though firmly gripping a steering wheel, he turned the corner, down-shifted, and slammed on the brakes in front of the teacher's desk. With a cocky grin and mischief in his eyes, he asked, "Dude, where's my desk? In the back of the room again this year?"*

> *Before driving away, he mused, "Hey, guess what? I dressed myself this morning!" Speeding towards his desk, the teacher noticed in one back pocket was a rolled-up comic book, in the other... his underwear.*
>
> *The teacher's thoughts now, "This is going to be a challenging year!"*

Now here's the point, and it applies to anyone in any form of leadership: Motivation must be as diverse as the group of people you lead. To think one approach fits all is foolish and sets the stage for a downward spiral of frustration and failure. The little guy with the briefcase would need a much different approach than the little guy with the underwear in his back pocket.

Though there has to be a plan to meet the needs of the overall team, there must also be a plan to meet the individual needs of those within the team. Without question, like building a solid foundation, it will take a tremendous amount of time, structure, consistency, and communication skills, but the rewards will be worth the effort.

Author and former presidential speechwriter James Humes, insists, "The art of communication is the language of leadership." Called the pioneer of the self-improvement industry, Paul J. Meyer believes, "Communication--the human connection--is the key to personal and career success." And Irish playwright, critic, and political activist George Bernard Shaw insisted, "The single biggest problem in communication is the illusion that it has taken place."

If there is but a shred of validity in any of these men's words, grip that steering wheel, down-shift, turn the corner, and start communicating--with everybody!

28

To lead a good life... look to the heavens wearing work boots.

To attain "beyond beautiful" results, hard-working influencers wake up and get ready to take on the world. They strap on their work boots, understanding million-dollar dreams become nothing more than fool's gold with a 25-cent work ethic.

29

To lead a good life... provide a single thread of hope.

To help someone on your team regain confidence, you must find a way to take that person back to the exact moment it was lost, set a methodical plan of attack, and diligently start over. Though humbling, it's an honest process, involving intense perseverance, unlimited patience, and a chance to change a life.

30

To lead a good life... put a little burst of sunshine in someone's day.

Treasure and savor the gift from within your heart called kindness. It holds tightly to the keys to your success. Taking that thought to a deeper, more personal level, offering kindness during another person's despair has the potential to prepare and lift both to greatness.

31

To lead a good life... grab a chair, any chair, and sit down.

Gifted leaders develop and maintain success with a blend of empowerment, inspiration, and cooperation. They believe elevating others broadens their influence and heightens their cause. They also realize fear stifles creativity, turning all thought inward and away from the goal.

32

To lead a good life... down shift and turn the corner.

Though there has to be a plan to meet the needs of the overall team, there must also be a plan to meet the individual needs of those within the team. It will take a tremendous amount of time, structure, consistency, and communication skills, but the rewards will be worth the effort.

33

To lead a good life…

Park the helicopter and "git out the way."

What a wonderful opportunity we have as teachers, coaches, mentors, and parents, to teach our children how to compete. Young people today have the same competitive dreams we had back in our day. The difference: when they compete, we tend to hover, swoop, and make all kinds of senseless noise, robbing our children of opportunities to enjoy the process, stand on their own two feet, and experience the fundamental lessons offered in competition. Thus, they are dubbed "helicopter parents."

As if hovering isn't enough, there's another term being used in the world of youth sports to describe controlling parents. They're referred to as "snow-plow parents." Their goal is to get out in front of their children and clear the road for their success. They'll spare no expense and use every tactic known to man to push aside anything that will hinder a smooth, uninterrupted ride to the top--and all semblance of true competition is cleared and readied for nothing more than token participation and unrealistic results. In the end, they're destined to become the same parents who can't understand why their sons and daughters fall apart when life's real challenges and adversities arise.

Though sometimes difficult, we must set aside our selfish agendas of pride and prestige, allowing our children to grow and develop as competitors. They may fall, skin a knee, make mistakes, or experience rejection, but the lessons learned without our meddling, will better prepare them for the real world.

Here's one example of a lost opportunity:

> *With head down, arms pumping, and heart racing, the little guy was rounding second and heading for third. The first-base coach, with hands cupped around his mouth and veins popping out of his neck, was screaming to get the 5-year-old turned around and headed back to second. The third-base coach had a different idea. As if directing a firetruck, he was windmilling one arm, pleading for the little guy to keep sprinting toward third.*
>
> *Confused, the baserunner stopped, put his head down, and started to cry. When tagged out, his coaches, his teammates, and the hometown crowd went into beast mode. As though leaning over the railing at a dog track, they were yelling at the first grader like he was a car thief. With a hard tug on the collar, the third-base coach drag/pulled the teary-eyed little guy into the dugout without uttering a word. Too busy trying to reign supreme, he never bothered to explain to the young man what went wrong--just win, baby.*

Now here are a few million-dollar questions to ponder: What did the young man learn? Do you think he enjoyed the experience? Do you suppose he's looking forward to his next base hit? Nope. Not a chance. At his age, he'd rather stay home and bury himself in cartoons and video games. Before it's too late, before our youth decide to hang up their spikes, we need to find well-intentioned coaches, turn the helicopter around, land it, store it, and walk away.

When a father grabs his son by the nape of the neck, drags him across a baseball field, and berates him for missing a tackle--in front of his teammates--excuse the poor English, but that ain't winnin'. When a mother rips into her daughter for spiking a volleyball into the net--in front of the hometown crowd--excuse me, but that ain't winnin'. And when a coach screams at a 5-year old for his lack of base-running skills--in front of his mom, his, dad, and his Uncle Joe--you guessed it, that ain't winnin'.

In one of his albums entitled *We Shall Overcome: The Seeger Sessions*, Bruce Springsteen, who has sold more than 135 million records worldwide, sings an old folk song, using the phrase, "git out the way, old Dan Tucker." In working with today's youth, we need to follow his advice and "git out the way," letting our children grow, develop, and stand on their own two feet. That, my friend, is winnin'.

34

To lead a good life…

Don't lose Johnny in the shuffle.

Observation has often been called "the education of leadership." Without observing those you lead--their work ethic, mannerisms, and social interactions--there's not much guidance in developing a team.

National columnist and author Marilyn vos Savant, who once scored the highest IQ ever recorded, wrote, "To acquire knowledge, one must study; to acquire wisdom, one must observe." As her intelligence quotient is probably much higher than yours and mine, I think Marilyn is probably worth listening to.

After some honest observation of his own, a veteran coach realized he dropped the ball in his attempt to develop an all-inclusive approach to building team chemistry. With good intentions, he called one of the captains up to share a valuable lesson about the power of observation:

> *The coach stood at one end of the weight room. His team stood at the other, waiting for the signal to start their workout. As he waited, he liked to observe his players interacting. In doing so, he could gauge his team's chemistry.*
>
> *On this day, he noticed something curious about one of his players: no one paid any attention to him. Like an old, forgotten statue, he stood alone. To avoid bringing attention to himself, he'd move from one spot to another, pretending to be involved. It was obvious, this wasn't the first time he went through this lonely routine. The coach could almost feel the young man's pain and wondered*

> *why he'd never noticed his loneliness before.*
>
> *Signaling for one of his captains, he asked, "How's our team chemistry?"*
>
> *"We're doing great, Coach!"*
>
> *"Everyone feeling like a vital part of the team?"*
>
> *"I think everybody's good, Coach."*
>
> *"Is that right? Watch Johnny over there and tell me if he's feeling included."*
>
> *After a short time observing the lonely player, the captain asked, "Coach, is it like this all the time?"*
>
> *"I think it is, let's make sure it doesn't happen again."*

Not only did the team get bigger, stronger, and faster in the weight room that day, there were a couple other, more valuable accomplishments:

- First, through honest observation, two of its leaders gained more knowledge of their team's chemistry.

- Second, with the wisdom acquired, it stimulated the process of making one of their own feel more valued and their team more complete--not a bad day's work.

When you bring your team together to educate, train, or inspire, as the process unfolds, don't forget to observe. Find your leaders, find your followers, and find those poor souls, like Johnny, lost in the shuffle. Then, using all available talents and resources, make them feel more valued and included. More than books, seminars, training, or experience, in the world of leadership, observation is the best team-building tool. It's a simple skill, but it's potential in developing a team, like finding a new source of energy, is off the grid. Charge it up.

35

To lead a good life…

Honor the hand-held timer.

A quick study of the word "integrity" reveals some of the following insights: A single lie, a moment of weakness, a touch of unfairness, or a convenient look-the-other-way, and an entire reputation can be destroyed. If you stay true to your word, are impeccable with your actions, and hold firm to what you know is right, you'll keep your good name and your family will be blessed with your virtue.

If you look closely, you'll find examples of integrity as you travel through life. Here's one of my favorites:

> *It was a freshman football game. Though not many people showed up for ninth-grade games, those who did were anxious to watch their teams compete. It wasn't Friday night under-the-lights, but those in attendance were proudly wearing their colors, excited to watch their sons compete on the varsity field.*
>
> *Like young Roman gladiators, each team battled hard to represent their school and their community. It was a smash-mouth game and the excitement reached a fevered pitch as they entered the final moments of play.*
>
> *With the home team behind by a few points, they were driving for the winning score. At the start of the fourth quarter, the scoreboard had a malfunction and the athletic director walked the field with a hand-held timer. As small-town luck would have it, his son was the quarterback for the team inching its way closer and closer to the goal line.*

> *With the ball resting on the one-yard line and time running out, the team hurried to the ball as the quarterback placed his hands under the center and started barking the cadence. Just before the ball moved, the father waved his arms and called, "Time!" Racing toward the line of scrimmage, the official immediately blew the whistle, signaling the end of the game.*

The ball was on the one-yard line... nobody in the stadium could see the time... and his son was under center ready to take the snap... but the father ended the game. For him, there would be no moment of weakness, no touch of unfairness, or convenient look-the-other-way. As a World War II veteran from "The Greatest Generation," he was more concerned with keeping the family name clean and teaching his son about doing things the right way.

With a complete understanding of the value of high school athletics and holding firm to what he knew was right, the father was content with the results of the game. Putting his hand-held timer in his pocket, he congratulated his son on a nice game and headed home. On this day, there would be no last-minute heroics, no victory, no celebration--just a firm handshake, a family blessing, and a solid lesson on honesty.

In your role as a leader, you can cheat, find loopholes, and win at all costs. Or, with the grace of the father trudging down the field, gripping his trusty hand-held timer, you can hold your team accountable, teach moral correctness, demonstrate integrity, and insist on fair play.

It's your call, the clock is ticking.

36

To lead a good life...

Take the test... without the answers.

Award-winning children's author, Emilie Buchwald, once wrote, "Children are made readers on the laps of their parents." And so it is with everything in a child's world. They have not yet been taught the destructive power of hatred, intolerance, racism, or prejudice, and they can't yet comprehend the positive impact of honesty, integrity, sympathy, or truth.

About all a young child knows is what they've been taught at home by those who brought them into this world. From within the confines of this fundamental truth, we have a wonderful opportunity to give our children the tools needed to grow, develop, thrive, and better understand our world.

In teaching and raising today's youth, speaker, author, and behavioral scientist Steve Maraboli offers the following advice: "What we instill in our children will be the foundation upon which they build their future."

Former University of Michigan head football coach Bo Schembechler's father, as though intentionally following Maraboli's advice, instilled a rock-solid foundation upon which Bo could build his future.

In his book, *Bo's Lasting Lessons*, the legendary coach tells a story about his dad, a fire captain in Barberton, Ohio, one of two candidates for fire chief:

> *My dad liked to go down to the local Elks Club and*

> *play cards with his buddies, some who were on the fire department, too. You know, small-town stuff. One day he shows up, one of his buddies' hands him a manila envelope, and tells him, "Here, this is for you."*
>
> *"What is it?"*
>
> *"It's the answers for the civil service exam."*
>
> *"Why are you giving it to me?"*
>
> *"Because the other guy already has them. It's only fair."*
>
> *"I can't do that," he said. He left. And when he came home, he cried. I'll never forget it.*

Bo's father took the test… without the answers, scoring in the high nineties. The other guy, the one with all the answers, scored higher--one or two points higher.

Though he never experienced his lifelong dream of being the chief and running his own fire station, by his own words and actions, he taught his son a valuable lesson about honesty. Refusing to compromise his core beliefs, to the dismay of Ohio State coach Woody Hayes and a host of other Big-Ten and NCAA coaches, he gave his son a foundation he could build his future upon--a college football, hall of fame foundation. Hail to the victor!

Sixty-nine-year-old, long-distance runner Anthony Gaskell knows about cheating and losing one's integrity. He set a record in the London Marathon for competitors over 65, finishing the race in the startling time of 3 hours and 5 minutes. The problem: he hopped a barrier, took off through the streets of London, and gifted himself a 10-mile shortcut.

Remember when Rosie Ruiz ran the Boston Marathon? Taking Gaskell's tactics to another level, she too ran a startling race and was the first woman to cross the finish line. The problem: as she basked in the limelight of an adoring crowd, the judges figured out good-old Rosie purchased a subway ticket, climbed aboard, took a seat, and comfortably rode beneath the city streets of Boston to the finish line.

Like Gaskell and Ruiz, in 2017 the Houston Astros General Manager Jeff Luhnow and field manager A. J. Hinch helped their team swindle its way to victory. Failing to prevent an elaborate, sign-stealing operation, they looked the other way, giving the Astros an edge in reading opposing pitchers. The two men lost their jobs, destroyed their legacies, and were ushered out of the game of baseball in disgrace.

It's just my opinion, but I have a feeling these misguided sports figures could've learned a thing or two from Bo Schembechler's dad. Had he schooled these flim-flam artists on the finer points of integrity, there would've been no barrier-hopping, subway-riding, sign-stealing, hot shots gnawing at the very fiber of the sports world.

Like I said, take the test... without the answers.

37

To lead a good life...

Search for people with Ph.D. qualities.

As a leader, it seems logical to surround yourself with good people. In doing so, it's easy to gravitate toward those with high IQ's, Ivy League degrees, and color-coded resumes. But before you get too enamored with test scores, GPA's, and leather briefcases, you might want to consider a different approach. Without people of commitment, forget about long-range success. Let's be honest, dedication, devotion, and loyalty are the forces that tether hope to achievement and action to accomplishment. As they say in the school of hard knocks, "Without commitment, you ain't goin' nowhere."

Here's an idea: When looking to add to your team or workforce, look for people with a Ph.D.--poor, hungry, and driven. I don't mean financially poor. I mean not yet discovered, those with skills that are raw, untapped, and pure. Like lonely Hollywood hopefuls, they crave hard work and discipline. They dream big, they're self-motivated, and they push themselves beyond common expectations. Oh, they're out there. You just gotta find 'em. Those who do will heighten their team's chances of success. Those who don't will grovel with the bottom feeders.

The young lady in the following story certainly has Ph.D. qualities:

> *When my older sister Karen was in high school, she was babysitting me and a couple of my brothers and sisters. She assured my parents she was dependable and promised them she'd do a good job. After putting us to bed, she invited a friend over to the house. They were in*

> *one of the upstairs bedrooms and Karen was styling her friend's hair.*
>
> *By chance, her friend was positioned directly in front of a window. Without warning, she let out an ear-popping scream. Peering in from just a few feet away, she could see a man's beady eyes staring directly back into hers.*
>
> *How did my sister respond? Did she retreat, hide under the bed, or wait for someone else to save the day? Nope. As though charging out of an Alabama locker room, she ran down the stairs, sprinted into the kitchen, grabbed a butcher knife, and bolted out the back door.*
>
> *Realizing he'd been discovered, the intruder leaped off the roof, scrambled to the back of the yard, and hid between a row of bushes and the neighbor's shed. With butcher knife in hand, Karen approached the prowler, bent down real low, stuck the knife out toward his face, and said, "You come out of there right now!"*
>
> *You never saw a man move so fast. As if shot out of a circus cannon, he flew across the neighbor's yard. With head back and arms pumping, he high-stepped into the night, never to be seen nor heard from again.*

Listen close, I'm not necessarily advocating hiring people who chase stalkers around their backyard with a butcher knife, and I know this is a pretty crazy example of being committed to the task at hand. But if you're looking to build a powerful team, I am advocating you search for people with some of my sister's Ph.D. qualities, giving them a chance to compete with the Ivy Leaguers flaunting their color-coded resumes.

For the record, there's a high-stepping circus clown out there somewhere who could verify the power of commitment.

33

To lead a good life... park the helicopter and, "git out the way."

Though sometimes difficult, we must set aside our own selfish agendas of pride and prestige, allowing our children to grow and develop as competitors. They may fall, skin a knee, make mistakes, or experience rejection, but the lessons learned, without our meddling, will better prepare them for the real world.

34

To lead a good life... don't lose Johnny in the shuffle.

When you bring your team together to educate, train, or inspire, as the process unfolds, don't forget to observe. Find your leaders, find your followers, and find those poor souls lost in the shuffle. Then, using all available talents and resources, make them all feel more valued and included.

35

To lead a good life... honor the hand-held timer.

A single lie or a moment of weakness, and an entire reputation can be destroyed. If you stay true to your word, are impeccable with your actions, and hold firm to what you know is right, you'll keep your good name and your family will be blessed with your integrity.

36

To lead a good life... take the test... without the answers.

About all a young child knows is what they've been taught at home by those who brought them into this world. From within the confines of this fundamental truth, we have a wonderful opportunity to give our children the tools needed to grow, develop, thrive, and better understand our world.

37

To lead a good life... search for people with Ph.D. qualities.

When looking to add to your workforce, look for people with skills that are raw, untapped, and pure. Find those who crave hard work and discipline, people who dream big, are self-motivated, and push themselves beyond common expectations.

38

To lead a good life...

Take time for a two-second handshake.

Our words, like a perfect storm, are one of the most powerful forces known to man. As leaders, we can use this energy constructively, or we can use it destructively. It's our choice, evolving from our own free will.

As though preaching from a church pulpit, we can use our words to encourage, praise, lift, and develop a connection of trust. Or, as though casting gossip from the gates of Hell, we can use them to hurt, harm, and humble, destroying any hope of bringing people together to work, create, accomplish, and celebrate success. In the end, our words, costing not one red cent, will define much of our happiness.

Spending a lifetime in coaching, I've preached from the pulpit of encouragement, and I've cast negative influence from the gates of Hell.

Allow me to share the positive. On the first day of varsity football practice, the young sophomore was hustling like crazy. I told him, in front of the entire squad, "Hey Ward, I like the way you hustle." Over 35 years later he still remembers the time, the drill, and the exact spot on the field I complimented him.

He once said to me, "I appreciated what you said in front of the team that day, Coach, it motivated me to work even harder."

That's it, one compliment and he was influenced for decades." By the way, he eventually became a coach on my staff. Not a bad return on a simple, one-sentence investment.

On the other side of the coin, I blasted a player in front of the entire team for being disrespectful during a team scrimmage. I went overboard, and I regret it to this day. He didn't talk to me for a long time. Why, because I lost my temper and embarrassed him. It went beyond constructive criticism. As a leader, I had a chance to approach the situation differently, use it as an opportunity to teach, influence, and lead, but I failed. For that, there's no excuse.

Here's another example of establishing positive communication skills and developing trust:

> *There were two retirement parties within a few weeks of each other. One was for a custodian; the other was for a high school principal. Though both men had different duties and responsibilities, their styles of communicating offer an interesting contrast in developing relationships and finding happiness.*
>
> *The custodian's party was a riot, jammed with people who respected him as a person and a co-worker. With the confidence of a true friend, he shared a personal, work-related story with everyone who came. Shedding tears of joy, they laughed together, they cried together, and they celebrated together. It was obvious, he'd spent a lifetime developing personal relationships with those he worked with and served. He seemed to be the happiest man on the planet.*
>
> *As if partying on the infield of the Indianapolis 500, the custodian's celebration continued through the night and into the wee hours of the morning. Nobody wanted to leave.*
>
> *The principal, however, had a different style of communicating. He was all about reigning power, keeping his distance, and hiding behind a strict chain of command. Like a pompous rock-star, he'd stroll out of his office, swagger down the hall, and nod his head a few times. As if reaching a familiar dead end, he'd grunt, turn around, and head right back to his office.*
>
> *As you'd guess, his retirement party was different. Much different. There weren't many personal stories or tears of joy, just a few forced smiles and an excess of nervous conversation. As if attending a wake, people came, paid their respects, and quietly eased out the back*

> *door. Like a punch-drunk fighter, the principal seemed lost and confused, paying a heavy price for his distant, impersonal approach.*

Though your retirement party might be a distant speck on the horizon, it'd be best to start preparing today. A simple word of encouragement, a short conversation about family and friends, or a two-second handshake is about all it takes to start developing a base of trust and caring. Certainly, there has to be warmth in your approach, and if your intentions come from the heart, you'll find your happiness, not in the millions you spend chasing it, but rather in the words you choose--costing less than one red cent.

39

To live a good life...

Create some beautiful family music.

Addressing a group of potential leaders, the speaker offered the following message: "A family is like music, some high notes, some low notes, but always a beautiful sound."

He continued, "Understand this, some people don't understand the team concept because they've never heard those beautiful family sounds. In creating a team, it's our job as leaders, to create the family music they've never heard."

To help verify his thoughts, the speaker shared the following story:

> *When the coach opened his office door, a distraught young man stood outside. Motionless, he was looking down at his hands as though his heart were resting on his palms--beating fast, pounding out of rhythm.*
>
> *In one cruel and unforgiving moment, his mother took the money he'd saved to get his college education started. With no regard for the sweet music of family, she spent it on drugs and alcohol. All of it! One long and selfish binge, and the money he'd saved waiting tables and working odd jobs, blended into nothingness.*
>
> *Desperately trying to compose himself, he said, "Coach, I need help, and I don't know where to turn."*
>
> *Before he left the office, they devised a new game plan for the young man's future. With the help of a few loyal friends, boosters, and business partners, they secured a safer place for him to live, a better paying job, a meeting with a local college counselor, and a little financial*

> support. *The young man was back on his feet, his dreams were still alive, and his heart was no longer racing out of control.*
>
> *Fast forward to about six years. The same kid knocked on the same door.*
>
> *"Coach, today I received my college degree. I stopped by to thank you for your help, but I need to ask just one last favor. I just got my first job and it will take me a few months to get on my feet and get situated. Once I do, if you have anyone on your team who needs help in any way, I want you to call me. I want to give back, Coach. I need to give back."*

In the young man's home, high notes were almost non-existent. Poor choices and addiction destroyed all harmony, silencing the beautiful sounds of family. He was fortunate to hear some of those sounds elsewhere.

A proud father once said, "A happy family is but an early heaven." If a person can't seem to reach, touch, or feel an early heaven, as leaders, we must answer the call for help. In doing so, we'll inspire new hope, afford opportunities to hear the beautiful sounds of family, and enhance a better understanding of a team. That's sweet music.

In the challenging sphere of influence, like a hard punch in the gut, sometimes life knocks you for a loop, making it harder and harder to let go of the gifts you've been blessed with. As many leaders would agree, it's healthy to sit down, reflect, and put your thoughts on paper... maybe even write yourself a poem. Who knows, maybe it'll give you the boost you need to continue to fight the good fight:

Let Go Your Gifts of Love

I've seen it in their haunted eyes,
They quickly look away.
It settles in their lifeless smiles,
Forgotten how to play.

I've recognized the pain and hurt,
As dreams all fade away.
It slows them in the way they walk,
Heads bowed as if to pray.

I've noted looks of helplessness,
The fear of mom or dad.
A desperate search for simple joys,
The life they wish they had.

Too many hearts are broken,
A haunting, vicious game.
A thousand dreams are shattered,
Each day it beats the same.

So many lives to save and keep,
Let go your gifts of love.
You'll help them rest and sleep at night,
Give wings to rise above.

Just bring it from your heart and soul,
They'll cherish what you say.
You'll feel it in the way they sing,
Help harmonize their day

You're blessed, take heed, be thankful,
You've shared your gifts of love.
The candle lit as hope evolves,
Gave wings to rise above.

-Tony Legando

40

To live a good life...

Don't worry about recognition, just serve.

I've often wondered, who benefits most from servant leadership? Is it the person serving or the one being served? In the end, I guess it doesn't matter much, as long as both roll up their sleeves and get the job done. After all, as they say in circles of higher expectations, "The most meaningful rewards are not what one receives for their work, they're found in what one becomes."

When Socrates served fellow philosopher Plato, he wasn't concerned with the rewards he'd receive for his service. He was more concerned with what the two philosophers could become.

How'd he do? Socrates had a profound influence on ancient and modern philosophy, and Plato is known today as the father of idealism in philosophy. In other words, as a mentor and servant leader, Socrates did pretty well.

When Warren Buffett served fellow businessman Bill Gates, he wasn't concerned with any recognition he'd receive for his service. He was more concerned with what the two businessmen could become.

How'd he do? Today Buffett is considered the most successful investor in the world and Gates is best known as the co-founder of Microsoft Corporation--the world's leading technology company. As a mentor and servant leader, it's safe to say Warren Buffet got the job done.

Like Socrates and Buffet, a teenager was summoned to roll up his sleeves and serve a fellow student, and the results reflected the benefits of servant leadership for all involved:

> *As the 60 young boys warmed up in the gym for their non-contact summer football camp, the coach noticed a father and son standing in the hallway. As if hiding, they were huddled together, peering out from behind a set of lockers. The child seemed excited. The dad seemed worried.*
>
> *The coach ventured out to introduce himself and asked if he could help.*
>
> *"Yes, my son has been talking about your camp for months. He really wants to be a part of it and join all the other boys. His mom and I aren't really sure he's ready for a camp like this."*
>
> *The coach recognized the young man from school, remembered he was a special-needs child, and said, "I'm a bit familiar with your son and understand your concerns. How about we give it a shot? I've got a lot of good help. We can have an upperclassman shadow him and make sure he's comfortable. I'm confident we can make this work and give your son a healthy experience."*
>
> *The coach had the perfect upperclassman in mind to follow the new camper, a young man who needed a boost of confidence and a feeling of belonging. It turned out to be a match made in heaven. The big kid had a job to do, an important job, and he was proud the coach picked him.*
>
> *At the end of the day, the coach noticed the father, in the same spot, hiding by the lockers, watching his son perform. This time, he didn't look worried; he looked proud and hopeful and happy. As the coach approached to let him know how well it worked out, the father shook his hand and thanked him for helping his child.*
>
> *Before they parted, the father asked, "Hey Coach, could I meet the young man who helped my son today? I watched him work. He's a great kid, Coach. He has no idea how much this means to my son and our family."*

On the last day of camp, the parents were invited to watch their sons demonstrate a few agility drills. As the whistle blew, the coach realized he forgot to match the special-needs child with his mentor.

When he found the little guy, he was pleased with what he saw. Following the youngster, step-by-step and all smiles was his servant leader. In watching the two, the coach wasn't sure who benefited most. But in the end, I guess it doesn't matter much, together, they were getting the job done.

41

To lead a good life...

Praise the Lord, just do the right thing.

In the throes of making a tough decision, people love to tell you, "Just do the right thing." People who say that make it sound so easy when in reality, doing the right thing can sometimes get you in a little hot water.

In 2001, Anne Mulcahy was named CEO and chairperson of Xerox. There was, however, one problem: In 2000, the company had lost $273 million dollars. When she took over the company, they were on the verge of bankruptcy and were $17 billion in debt.

How did she respond? Did she do the right thing for Xerox to survive? Immediately jumping into the hot water, one of her decisions was to let go of 22,000 loyal employees--not 20, 200, or 2,000. She let go of 22,000.

The results of her making tough decisions were staggering. In 2003--are you ready for this--the company recorded a $91 million profit.

If you want to lead, inspire, and motivate others, regardless of the consequences, you must be willing to jump in the hot water and confront the problem. You might not want to get involved, but if you're going to be a person of influence... ya' gotta do it.

The teacher in the story below didn't have to deal with 22,000 loyal employees, but he was responsible for educating his students, and he was willing to do the right thing to enhance their experience:

| *The new fourth-grade, Catholic school teacher was* |

excited about his first job. Determined to make a difference in the lives of his students, he was ready to dig in, accept his challenges, and... "just do the right thing."

Before taking his class to the school library to return their books, he decided to talk to the librarian. After his last visit, he could see she sometimes intimidated his students, and he wanted to address the issue. He knew the conversation might create a bit of a firestorm, but he stopped in to talk to her anyway.

"Excuse me, I was wondering if I could talk to you for a minute?"

A bit irritated, the librarian responded, "Sure, but make it quick. I've got a lot to do."

"Oh, okay, I just wanted to make sure we're on the same page. Some of the children in my class are really nervous about coming to the library today. In fact, a couple had a few tears in their eyes. They forgot their books, and they're really worried about it. As their reading teacher, I want them to enjoy coming to the library. Is there a way we can work together to be sure it's always a positive experience?"

In disbelief, she tilted her head, tightened her jaw, and scolded, "Well, I feel like I've just been disrespected. I quit!"

As if being excommunicated from the church, she grabbed her purse, three crossword puzzle booklets, and a coffee mug. As she passed, she put her nose in the air, mumbled something about a cardinal sin, and bolted out the door.

With his tail tucked tightly between his legs, the new teacher headed for the principal's office, certain he was the one about to be excommunicated.

"Excuse me, Sister, can we talk?"

When he explained what happened, she asked, "The librarian did what?"

"I'm sorry, Sister, she quit."

After an uncomfortable pause, the principal leaned forward, looked at him over the top of her glasses, and whispered, "Praise the Lord, we've been trying to get rid of her for a long, long time. Thank you!"

When we meet the enemy and we can see the whites of their eyes, we have to make one of those tough, leadership decisions. We can allow those poor souls of gloom and doom to invade our space, make us miserable, and control our destiny. Or, we can have one of those come-to-Jesus moments, make sure they see the whites of our eyes and, praise the Lord, "just do the right thing."

Made it sound easy, didn't I? But if you're going to lead, impact, and influence others... ya' gotta do it!

38

To lead a good life… take time for a two-second handshake.

A simple word of encouragement, a short conversation about family and friends or a two-second handshake is about all it takes to start developing a base of trust and caring. There has to be a consistency of purpose, but if your intentions come from the heart, you'll find your happiness.

39

To lead a good life… create some beautiful family music.

A family is like music, some high notes, some low notes, but always a beautiful sound. Some people don't understand the team concept because they've never heard those beautiful family sounds. In creating a team, it's our job as leaders, to create the family music they've never heard.

40

To lead a good life… don't worry about recognition, just serve.

In achievement, it doesn't matter who gets the credit, as long as everyone rolls up their sleeves and gets the job done. As they say in circles of higher expectations, "The most meaningful rewards are not what one receives for their work, they're found in what one becomes."

41

To lead a good life… praise the Lord, just do the right thing.

When we meet the enemy, we have to make one of those tough, leadership decisions. We can allow those poor souls to invade our space, make us miserable, and control our destiny. Or, we can have one of those come-to-Jesus moments and make sure we just do the right thing.

Part 3

Motivation

"I've got a dream that's worth more than sleep."
Anonymous

"It's a slow process, but quitting won't speed it up."
Anonymous

"Motivation is what gets you started. Habit is what keeps you going."
Entrepreneur Jim Rohn

"I survived because the fire inside me burned brighter than the fire around me."
Anonymous

"I have an everyday religion that works for me. Love yourself first, and everything else falls into line."
Actress Lucille Ball

"Everyone motivates, until they get kicked in the teeth."
Anonymous

"All right. They're on our left, they're on our right, they're in front of us, they're behind us... they can't get away this time."
Marine Corps Lieutenant General Lewis "Chesty" Puller

42

To lead a good life…

Forget the 8-hour workday.

Here's a revelation: Table salt isn't very expensive. Walk into your local grocery store and check it out. Twenty-six ounces of Morton Iodized Table Salt will cost you about 84 cents. Pretty cheap, right? I don't shop much, but it sounds pretty cheap to me.

What about talent? How expensive is talent? In pure dollars and cents, it's about as expensive as--take a deep breath--the air you breathe. That's it!

American author Stephen King connected the analogy when he said, "Talent is cheaper than table salt." But he didn't stop there, adding, "What separates the talented individual from the successful one is a lot of hard work." Obviously, Mr. King had a handle on what you need to succeed in life, he's worth about $400 million.

In the short passage below, from *Developing the Leader from Within You*, author John C. Maxwell tries to convince his readers, hard work, not talent, is the cornerstone for building a foundation of success:

> *Imagine where we would all be today if some of the greatest people the world has ever known wouldn't have invested in hard work. Where would we be in our understanding of space if Neil Armstrong, the first man to walk on the moon, had never finished the grueling training of being an astronaut? Imagine our world today if Nelson Mandela, the man who negotiated the end of apartheid in South Africa, worried about an eight-hour workday. Where would our country be if Thomas*

> *Jefferson, the principal author of the Declaration of Independence, wasn't an enthusiastic student, sometimes spending 15 hours a day in deep thought and study? And what would the world of music have missed if Mozart, one of the most prolific and influential composers of the classical period, hadn't been diligent in studying other great composers of his time?*

Thankfully, our world is a better place to live in because those accomplished individuals understood hard work is what separates the talented individual from the successful one. As a knowledgeable influencer once said, "They are men and women of ordinary talent, who submerged themselves in extraordinary hard work and perseverance, understanding the combination of both makes all things possible."

Dashrath Manjhi, also known as 'Mountain Man,' didn't believe in the 8-hour workday. His reputation was found, not in his talents, but rather in his work ethic.

As legend has it, Manjhi was a common laborer in Bihar, India. For 22 years, he single-handedly carved a path 360 feet long, 30 feet wide, and 25 feet deep. He didn't cut his path through a rocky ridge of hills with dynamite, earthmovers, and bulldozers. As if preparing for a paragraph or two in *Ripley's Believe It or Not*, from morning till night, he used nothing more than a hand-held hammer and a simple chisel.

Why? It's believed his wife had fallen from a steep ledge and died because he couldn't get her to the hospital in time. Though mocked for his crazy idea, when he finished digging, he'd shortened the path from 34 miles down to 3, and the same people who scorned his idea had quicker and easier access to the hospital.

Though the road to success is long and hard and sometimes littered with U-turns, roadblocks, and stop signs, people like Armstrong, Mandela, Jefferson, Mozart, and Mountain Man, prepared themselves for the long haul. They kept their foot on the gas and their eyes on their destination. They didn't let worries about talent, or the lack thereof, detour their travel.

When you're in doubt of reaching your own destination, or you find yourself lost in pursuit, forget about talent, simply reinvest in hard work. The total cost of that investment, less than 84 cents. The potential reward, about $400 million.

43

To lead a good life...

Respect your family journey.

Two guys walk into a barbershop. One's wearing a coat, tie, white shirt, dress pants, and spit-shined shoes. The other is wearing work clothes, covered head-to-toe with coal dust. Question: Who's more successful? Answer: The man who takes better care of his family. End of the discussion.

If we research our heritage, we'd find many of our ancestors had a very down-to-earth dress code. They found their success digging coal, emptying ships, pounding steel, or tilling soil. To take care of their families, they did some back-breaking, mind-bending, yeoman-like work. Covered with dirt, dust, grease, or oil, their days were so tough and their nights were so short, they didn't have time to dream about themselves. Their dreams were more about their sons and daughters, living a better, safer, and more prosperous life, steeped in the American Dream.

If we took the time to look back and appreciate the journey of our bloodlines, perhaps our workdays would be filled with more reverence and appreciation of our own journey.

In the passage below, you can't help but respect the journey:

> *In a coal mining town in Panther, WV, thin, horizontal slits were dug deep into the side of a nearby mountain. With nothing more than a hand-shovel, each hole was made long enough and wide enough to accommodate just one man, lying on his side. It was a claustrophobic squeeze, but when the work-whistle blew, each man, with*

> *shovel held tight to his chest, rolled into his dark, lonely place of work, ready to dig for coal--some only fourteen years old*
>
> *Always on his side, each miner chipped and scraped the coal with his shovel, awkwardly hefting it over his shoulder and into a bucket, lowered from above. When the bucket felt heavy against his back, he'd tug on the rope, waiting for it to be hauled up, emptied, and returned.*
>
> *This scenario played out all day, every day, for hours on end. The working conditions were tragic, the pay was poor, and the physical toll it took on their bodies was predictable. But these were tough men, hungry men, determined to put food on their table.*

One of the fourteen-year-old miners grew up and had eight children. His dreams were of each getting their education, moving away from the mines, and finding a safer, more comfortable existence. As chance would have it, one migrated to Huron, Ohio, and became a successful, high school basketball coach. His name was Jesse Hagy.

Much different from his father's work attire, Coach Hagy walked the sidelines with a coat, tie, white shirt, dress pants, and spit-shined shoes. He always had a prideful look, for he knew his family's success was paved with black dust and buckets of coal. With reverence and appreciation, he respected his family journey and used it as a motivator to take care of his own. It's called success. End of the discussion.

44

To lead a good life...

Honor a soldier, today.

Like oxygen to the lungs, we need freedom. Yet, do we take the time to honor, respect, and give thanks to those who've risked life and limb to help secure it? Or, are we content to offer a little Fourth-of-July lip-service, hit the beach, and hoist a glass in pretentious celebration of their service?

If we experienced the perils of war ourselves, parachuted into the night on foreign soil behind enemy lines and under heavy bombardment, would we approach all soldier celebration and remembrance differently? Just asking.

Many men and women, long after the battles fade and the blood dissolves, still pay a heavy price. Scarred, crippled, forever tired, and battle-weary, they are living symbols of freedom's cost. Yet, we take but one of 365 days to truly give thanks and honor their courage. The least we can do, as in the celebration presented below, is make that day special:

> *Every 4th of July, the Toledo Symphony Concert Band performs on the front porch of former President Rutherford B. Hayes' home in Fremont, Ohio. One of the last songs played is Tchaikovsky's powerful "1812 Overture." The song highlights a dramatic climax, with the firing of cannons in perfect time with the music.*
>
> *When the large guns erupt, you can feel the power of each blast resonating throughout the estate. The smoke and fire, exploding from the barrel of each cannon, is an*

> *up-close and personal reminder of the potential death and destruction of war.*
>
> *Feeling the force and hearing each blast echoing off the trees, are stark reminders of the courage and discipline required for soldiers to charge into harm's way. As the smoke drifts through the trees and blankets the ground, you can't help but feel a deep sense of appreciation for the young men and women serving our country.*

Walking away from the concert, I'm sure those in attendance wonder what motivates a person to conquer their fears? What drives a soldier to overcome the horror of death? What drives children to fight through the terror of emotional and physical abuse? What impels a person to get up early every morning, look deep into the eyes of death, and continue to battle a life-threatening disease?

We all know the answer is found in words like strength and courage and faith. But how do we reach and maintain the fortitude to continue the fight?

Here's what I've witnessed from people who have succeeded in doing so:

- First, they believe their lives are worthy of the fight.

- Second, they know nothing can destroy their character, their integrity, or their good name, and they refuse to let their situation compromise the gift of each.

- Third, they have a cause, something to fight for--the desire to get back home to see family and friends, the opportunity to defend a belief, a faith, or a principle.

- Fourth, the cause burns so deep inside their soul, with the fearlessness of a conqueror, they attack the challenge.

- Fifth, and this one seems to rise above all others, they use their fight to build a powerful legacy, understanding their fight will embolden others.

There's another song played earlier in the concert at the home of Rutherford B. Hayes. It's a medley representing each branch of the armed forces. As the band plays their respective song, the veteran of that branch stands to be recognized. Watching each proud soldier rise, and seeing the reactions of their family and friends, gives those in attendance a glimpse of the sheer beauty of what Independence Day is really all about--honoring those men and women who have somehow conquered their fears, ensured our freedom, and left a legacy to embolden others.

One day of 365 just doesn't seem enough to honor men and women who reached the highest levels of strength and courage and faith. Have you thanked a soldier, today? Just asking.

45

To lead a good life...

Shave half your head if you have to, but don't give up.

Remember the guy who gave up? That's okay, neither does anyone else. When some are tested, they throw in the towel and drift off into anonymity, eventually hanging with a league of malcontents. Others meet their challenges head-on, using their towel, not as a sign of surrender, but rather to wipe the sweat from their brow before continuing their pursuit.

If history has taught us anything about mental toughness it is this: As though you have wings, a little moxie can lift you to new heights; like an anvil in water, a little fear can drop you to new lows.

Professor James J. Murphy, in his book *On the Crown,* offers some insights into the persistence of a legendary orator:

> *Greek statesman Demosthenes had a tough childhood. He was born sick and frail with a traumatic speech impediment, making him an easy target for his peers. At age seven, he lost his father, leaving him with guardians who stole his entire inheritance. Making life even tougher, he was painfully shy and extremely awkward.*
>
> *Desperately wanting to fit in, Demosthenes would try anything to overcome his speech impediment. He enunciated words with pebbles in his mouth, shouted into the wind while running, and recited verse over the pounding of waves. Refusing to be denied, he tried reciting entire speeches in a single breath and once shaved half his head to force himself to stay inside and*

| *practice.* |

What were the results of Demosthenes' diligence and mental toughness? He proved adversity is like a controlled burn. The fire deadens, but the plants return more vibrant and colorful than before. Though the process was a constant uphill battle, his toughness lifted him to new and exciting heights. Considered the greatest lecturer of ancient Greece, he's called by some the "perfect orator who lacked nothing."

Ever hear of Ronald Wayne? Probably not. He gave up. About 40 years ago he was a co-founder of Apple. Having numerous arguments and disputes with the other founders, he sold his 10% of the company for--you ready for this--$800. Apple is worth about $1 trillion today. Expensive arguments!

How about Chris-Hill Scott, ever hear of him? Probably not. He gave up, too. He was a co-founder of SwiftKey. Long-hours and low pay did him in, trading his shares for--you ready for this--a bicycle. About eight years later, Microsoft acquired SwiftKey for $250 million. Expensive bike.

You want success, shout into the wind, shave half your head, or enunciate words with pebbles in your mouth if you have to... but don't give up. With a little moxie, stay true to yourself, wipe the sweat from your brow, and don't trade your bike for a few shares of stock. Just keep pedaling in pursuit of greatness. You'll get there.

46

To lead a good life…

Put pen to paper, make a day, change a life.

German theologian, mystic, and philosopher, Meister Eckhart, preached, "If the only prayer you ever say in your entire life is thank you. It will be enough." In *Table Talk for Family Fun*, author Martin Buxbaum shares a letter a minister sent to one of his former teachers. Some thirty years earlier, she opened his eyes to his potential and made him believe he could achieve it.

Realizing the heights of greatness reached and kept could not be attained alone, the minister decided to thank her for her part in his journey. One week after sending the letter, he received the following shaky, handwritten letter:

> *"My dear Willie: I want you to know what your note meant to me. I am an old woman in my eighties, living alone in a small room, cooking my own meals, and seeming like the last leaf on the tree. You will be interested to know, Willie, that I taught school for fifty years and in all that time, yours is the first letter of appreciation I have ever received. It came on a cold, blue morning and cheered my lonely old heart as nothing has cheered me in many years."*

The minister's handwritten letter of appreciation took but a few minutes to create, yet in that short amount of time, it was enough to make her happy and renew her spirit. Writing a letter or sending a simple note of thanks is about all it takes to make someone's day, make their life's work seem more valuable, or perhaps even change their life.

Neil Armstrong, the first man on the moon, took the time to write a thank you letter to the Extravehicular Mobility Unit, marking the 25th anniversary of the moon landing. The EMU gang, as he called them, built a spacesuit that kept him safe and alive while walking on the moon. The last sentence of his short letter summed up his feelings when he wrote, "To all of you who made it all it was, I send you a quarter century's worth of thanks and congratulations."

After his presidency, Ronald Reagan wrote a passionate letter of thanks to the American people. In the first sentence of his short letter, he wrote, "I have recently been told that I am one of millions of Americans who will be afflicted with Alzheimer's disease." In finishing, he wrote, "I now begin the journey that will lead me to the sunset of my life. I know that for America there will always be a bright dawn ahead. Thank you, my friends. May God always bless you."

Perhaps today, if you have a few minutes to spare, like Armstrong, Reagan, and Willie, thank someone who accepted you when you were at your worst, opened your eyes to what you could become, refused to accept your indifference, or pushed you beyond your wildest dreams.

Though putting pen to paper to write a note of thanks is a simple task of little effort, if it's all you ever do for that person, it'll be enough.

Review: Stories 42 - 46

42
To lead a good life... forget the 8-hour workday.

A plant without water is like talent without hard work. Neither will bear quality fruit. Although talent is a wonderful gift from above, invest in hard work and the fruits of your labor will be plentiful.

43
To lead a good life... respect your family journey.

With reverence, look back and appreciate your family journey. Your ancestors' days were so tough and their nights were so short, they didn't have time to dream about themselves. Their dreams were to make a better life for you. Use their journey as a motivator to work hard and take care of your own family.

44
To lead a good life... honor a soldier, today.

If we experienced the perils of war ourselves, parachuted into the night on foreign soil behind enemy lines, and under heavy bombardment, would we approach all soldier celebration and remembrance differently? I think so.

45
To lead a good life... shave half your head if you have to, but don't give up.

If history has taught us anything about mental toughness it is this: As though you had wings, a little moxie can lift you to new heights; like an anvil in water, a little fear can drop you to new lows.

46
To lead a good life... put pen to paper, make a day, change a life.

Thank someone who accepted you when you were at your worst, opened your eyes to what you could become, refused to accept your indifference, or pushed you beyond your wildest dreams. If it's all you ever do for that person, it'll be enough.

47

To lead a good life...

Astonish... even yourself.

There was a young man known throughout the world for his diligence, work ethic, and technical genius. As luck would have it, he was born just a few miles from my home in Huron, Ohio. He believed, "If we did all the things we are capable of doing, we'd literally astonish ourselves."

His name was Thomas Alva Edison and his accomplishments are well documented and familiar to most. Described as America's greatest inventor, he was a pioneer in the world of electric power generation, mass communication, sound recording, and motion pictures. I think it's safe to assume Mr. Edison, of Milan, Ohio, knew a little bit about accomplishment.

In his book entitled, *What Makes the Great Great*, author Dennis Kimbro convinces his readers, Booker T. Washington knew a little bit about accomplishment as well:

> *One day Mr. Washington, founder of Tuskegee Institute, encouraged a struggling student to stay in school. He told him the greatest accomplishments in life come with the highest of costs, assuring him, to achieve greatness, you must "pay the price of yourself."*
>
> *Booker T. asked the young man, "To reach success, will you shine shoes during the day and study Latin late into the night? Will you walk miles to borrow books you cannot afford? As you have no money to buy those books, are you ready to memorize your lessons? And how long*

> *will you toil to perfect your craft?"*
>
> *The teacher explained how freedom fighter Nat Turner laughed at death, and how abolitionist Harriet Tubman repeatedly used every fiber of her body to give freedom to others on the Underground Railroad. Challenging the young man, he assured him: success is nothing more than the "offspring of drudgery," and a man must be "self-made before he is ever made."*

Booker T. Washington, like Edison, understood and experienced the rewards of hard work. He also knew how to motivate his students. Using relative, historical examples he made it clear, to bring new light to a world sometimes cloaked in darkness, you must pay a heavy price, expect drudgery, and embrace different levels of discipline. Without each, the dreams of reaching exciting levels of accomplishment will die hard, leaving nothing more than the remorse of missed opportunities, the hurt of broken promises, and the pain of deep regret.

Of honest accomplishment, perhaps Mark Twain, hailed as America's finest humorist, said it best, "There are basically two types of people. People who accomplish things, and people who claim they accomplished things. The first group is less crowded." Booker T. Washington encouraged his students to be part of the first group.

Men and women of unparalleled achievement understand, for every worthwhile accomplishment, regardless of its size, its nature, or its historical significance, both failure and triumph must be met, endured, and eventually overcome.

If you're strong enough to follow the lead of people like Booker T. Washington and Thomas Alva Edison, you'll have the tools necessary to astonish… even yourself.

48

To lead a good life...

Chase those Golden Plovers.

Take a minute and let this anonymous quote sink in: "Those crazy enough to think they can make a difference in the world are usually the ones who do." Like crazed dogs, they attack their future with a vengeance, creating a life that gives them the incentive to get up early every morning and chase those crazy dreams. And here's the kicker, they seem to be the proudest people on the planet. Go figure.

Award-winning travel author Lee Foster, mesmerized by the grit and determination of the Polynesian quest to find land in the open seas of the Pacific Ocean, shared some of the following information in an article entitled *Hawaii's Hokulea Canoe Tells Story of the Polynesian Voyage*:

> *Marquesas Island is one of the many Polynesian Islands in the Pacific Ocean. It is 2,500 miles from Hawaii. No other island is closer. In today's world of high-tech navigation and travel, it takes about 30 days to sail from the remote islands of Marquesas to the lush paradise of Hawaii.*
>
> *Around 1,000 AD, using carved wooden boats and some crude navigational devices, the Polynesians discovered Hawaii. It took them 400 years! Not 4 years, not 40 years, but 400 years of dedication, determination, and faith.*
>
> *The Polynesians never really knew Hawaii was out there, but they suspected land somewhere because they*

> saw Golden Plover birds migrating north each year out
> into open seas. Dedicating themselves to reaching their
> unknown destination, they paddled hard, determined to
> keep up with the birds. Though they could only keep up
> for short distances, they eventually lost sight of the
> Golden Plovers and reluctantly turned back. Venturing
> out further each year, they kept the faith and finally
> reached Hawaii.

One can only imagine what the haters and naysayers on Marquesas Island thought when their countrymen, year after year, ventured further and further out into open waters, chasing migrating birds. Refusing to be deterred, they continued to dedicate themselves to finding a distant, undiscovered land.

As if chasing his own Golden Plovers, Charles Darwin, in the face of intense criticism and doubt, wasn't deterred. He started writing about his controversial theory of evolution in the late 1830s, but his book wasn't published until 1859.

Isaac Newton refused to back down from his challenges. He struggled for years to find himself, failing miserably as both a student and a farmer. Yet, he persisted in making a difference in the world, eventually becoming one of the most influential scientists the world has ever known.

And what about Elizabeth Blackwell? She didn't let intense criticism and gender discrimination stop her from being the first female in America to receive a degree in medicine. Despite the widespread opposition to her attending medical college, to the dismay of many, she finished first in her class.

Offering a clever message to those who doubt, and boldly encouraging dreamers not to be swayed by those who do, an unnamed letter writer offered the following words of wisdom: "Dear Haters, I have so much more for you to be mad at. Just be patient."

If you want to make a difference in the world, attack the Golden Plover challenges in your life and enjoy your happiness. As you go, be patient, the doubters, the haters, and the naysayers will be sure to follow. Go figure.

49

To lead a good life...

Realize your climb will define you.

"Mountain climbers, though worn and tired, get their best views from the steepest and most difficult climbs." At first glance, this often-used quote appears to be about the simple beauties and rewards of reaching the crest of a mountain. The intention, however, is more about inspiring those blinded by the darkness of adversity.

Like a boxer knocked off his feet and onto the canvas floor, leaders must regain focus, get up, and continue to fight, knowing the best education is found in triumph over struggle, and the climb will define them. American writer Kurt Vonnegut was knocked off his feet and onto the canvas floor a number of times. Yet, as in the passage below, he got up off his back and continued to fight:

> *His mother battled mental illness, was addicted to drugs and alcohol, and committed suicide on Mother's Day. He was captured by the Germans in World War II, was forced to work long hours in a malt-syrup factory, and slept in a subterranean slaughterhouse, exhuming corpses from the rubble of smoldering buildings.*
>
> *After surviving the Allied bombing in Dresden, in which tens of thousands of people were killed, he was forced to remove jewelry from the corpses before they were cremated. As mental illness was in his bloodline, he too battled deep bouts of depression. Like his mother, he tried to commit suicide by overdosing on alcohol and drugs. And there were more struggles. Many more.*

There are great benefits found within adversity. They will not reveal themselves, however, until one is tested and answers the call. Though tragic, physical abuse, mental illness, financial hardships, loneliness, and abandonment--to name just a few--tender unexpected strengths, releasing untapped resources of spirit and resolve.

Every loss, every disappointment, and every hardship, offers lessons in growth, improvement, and perseverance. Within heartache and distress, the seeds of advantage are sewn, demanding you plow deep within your soul to uncover them.

To our advantage, visions of great men and women struggling against adversity are some of the most inspiring sights this world has to offer.

Irish novelist James Joyce, energized by the struggle of a man's adversity, once said, "Your battles inspired me--not the obvious material battles but those that were fought and won behind your forehead."

There's a beautiful, faith-filled quote written by a man who published 14 novels, three collections of short stories, five plays, and five works of nonfiction. As though enjoying the view from atop a mountain after a hard climb, he offered the following advice on understanding, accepting, and finding peace in adversity: "Be soft. Do not let the world make you hard. Do not let pain make you hate. Do not let the bitterness steal your sweetness. Take pride that even though the world may disagree, you still believe it to be a beautiful place." The writer's name... Kurt Vonnegut--and his climb defines him.

50

To lead a good life...

Drench yourself in service, sacrifice, and respect.

Expensive cars, beautiful homes, and stylish clothes can certainly put a smile on your face and add an extra step in your giddy-up. But do they make you happy over the long haul? While you're thinking it over, consider this: President Richard Nixon, NFL Hall of Famer O.J. Simpson, Tour de France winner Lance Armstrong, and comedian Bill Cosby had it all. Drenched in money, power, fame, and success, it appeared they cornered the market on happiness. Somewhere in their rise to the top, however, they lost their focus, experiencing a painful fall from grace.

It's often been said, "The happiest people in the world are those who serve others." And when you meet them, you can't help it, as with the young man in the passage below, you like them right away:

> Joe was a senior in high school. He waited his entire football career to start for the team he loved and served. Now, it was his time.
>
> As an elementary student, he was an equipment boy, showing up every day at practice to do what he could to help the varsity. On game nights, he hauled equipment, served as a water boy, and made sure everyone had what they needed. He paid his dues and was ready to play under the lights on Friday nights.
>
> There was, however, one problem. A sophomore coming into the program played the same position as Joe, and he was good. Real good. After the first few practices,

> *the sophomore moved ahead of Joe on the depth chart, and the loyal senior became his backup.*
>
> *How did he respond? Did he become a negative force, or did he stay positive and put the team first? You decide.*
>
> *When the sophomore walked into the number one huddle for the first time, Joe was right behind him. When the team broke the huddle, Joe walked to the line of scrimmage with him, making sure the young player knew what to do. He coached the sophomore, every play, every day until the underclassman understood the intricacies of the position.*

Joe's legacy wasn't built on a foundation of tackles, catches, or points scored. His was built from within, on a quieter, more personal platform of service, sacrifice, and respect. Though he didn't have the power, the fame, or the high-profile success of a president, a world-class athlete, or a well-known entertainer, from within his place on a small high school football team, he never lost focus on the value of serving others. Refusing to make selfish decisions, there would be no painful falls from grace for Joe. He had too much class for that--tough kid, powerful legacy.

By the way, if you're ever in Marblehead, Ohio, and you're looking for a place to eat, stop by Netty's. It's the bright orange, old-fashioned hot dog stand right across from Danbury High School. The guy who owns the place, he seems to have cornered the market on being happy. His name is Joe. He has an easy smile and if you meet him, I guarantee you'll like him right away.

51

To lead a good life...

Make that kick in the teeth a distant, fading memory.

Albert Einstein, the funny looking guy who took a mind-bending theory and turned it into a usable mathematical equation, was a genius of simplicity. When asked his thoughts on adversity, as in matters of relativity, he didn't disappoint, insisting, "Adversity introduces a man to himself."

Like most deep thinkers, Einstein understood, when tested, you must delve deep inside your gut to find your core strength. In doing so, your ambitions will be inspired, your confidence will be elevated, and your fears will be controlled.

Though hard to endure, with the right attitude, a kick in the teeth may become nothing more than a distant, fading memory and a powerful gift to the soul. In the end, like steel to fire, you'll be tempered to rise up and tower above all challenges--with mind-bending results.

It's just my theory, but I believe Einstein would have been impressed with French journalist Jean-Dominique Bauby's ability to handle adversity. He suffered a stroke, disconnecting his brain from his spinal cord, leaving him a quadriplegic and a mute. Communicating with his eyelids, he published his memoirs entitled *The Diving Bell and the Butterfly*. It was published two days before he died of pneumonia.

Delving deep inside his soul, Bauby gathered his core strength and soared above his challenges, making them nothing more than weak and fading echoes from his past. In an article entitled *Benefits of*

Struggle in Life, Dr. Rekha Ramankutty offers an interesting lesson on adversity. By chance, as with Bauby's book, it involves a butterfly:

> *A man found the cocoon of a butterfly and noticed a tiny opening at one end. Observing the butterfly struggling to get out, he decided to speed the process. With a pair of scissors, he made the hole bigger. In awe, he watched the butterfly emerge without a struggle. Getting a closer look, to his dismay, he noticed the butterfly's body was swollen. Even worse, its wings were shriveled and wouldn't open.*
>
> *Sadly, the butterfly never flew. It spent the rest of its life crawling. What the man didn't understand was the importance of a butterfly's struggle in getting through the small opening of a cocoon. As it squeezes, fluid is forced throughout its wings, making it ready for flight.*

Author Randi G. Fine, a dedicated pioneer in abuse awareness, insists, "When life places a wall in our path we have two choices… we can beat our heads against it, or we can figure out a way to get around it." Einstein, Bauby, and Fine all recognized, in conflict we develop toughness, and in toughness, we find success--a hard journey, promising a smooth destination.

Imagine being charged to build the Panama Canal. You've prepared yourself to face the challenges of engineering, clean drinking water, sewage disposal, and organization, but you didn't plan to meet the challenges of flooding, yellow fever, malaria, and mosquitos. Would you beat your head against the wall of these challenges? Or, would you follow Randi G. Fine's advice and figure out how to get around them?

Imagine being commissioned to build the Transcontinental Railroad. You know your work will be long, hard, and dangerous, and you've prepared yourself to meet those challenges. You also know you'll have to build bridges over raging rivers, blast tunnels through steep mountains, navigate rugged ravines, and trudge across endless desert sands. But what you weren't really prepared for was hostile Native Americans attacking your workers, roaming buffalo impeding your progress, the never-ending threat of extreme weather conditions, and a multitude of deadly diseases.

When facing these setbacks, would you beat your head against a wall? Or, would you follow the lead of Jean-Dominique Bauby, dig deep into your soul, find your core strength, and, like a hunted eagle, soar above your challenges?

Review: Stories 47 - 51

47
To lead a good life... astonish... even yourself.

For every worthwhile accomplishment, regardless of its size, its nature, or its historical significance, both failure and triumph must be met, endured, and eventually overcome. If you're strong enough to follow the lead of people like Booker T. Washington and Thomas Alva Edison, you'll have the tools necessary to rise above your own expectations.

48
To lead a good life... chase those Golden Plovers.

Those crazy enough to think they can make a difference in the world are usually the ones who do. Like crazed dogs, they attack their future. With a vengeance, they create a life that gives them the incentive to get up early every morning and chase those crazy dreams. And here's the kicker, they seem to be the proudest people on the planet. Go figure.

49
To lead a good life... realize your climb will define you.

When blinded by the darkness of adversity, like a boxer knocked off his feet and onto the canvas floor, a leader must regain focus, get up off his back, and continue to fight, knowing the best education is found in triumph over struggle.

50
To lead a good life... drench yourself in service, sacrifice, and respect.

It's often been said, "The happiest people in the world are those who serve others." And when you meet them, you can't help it, you like them right away.

51

To lead a good life... make that kick in the teeth a distant, fading memory.

When tested, you must delve deep inside your gut to find your core strength. In doing so, your ambitions will be inspired, your confidence will be elevated, and your fears will be controlled.

52

To lead a good life...

Surprise even your mother-in-law.

Here's an understatement: "Walt Disney was a genius driven by a powerful imagination." Having a knack for seeing what others couldn't imagine, where they saw nothing more than farm animals and barnyards, he saw conversation, storylines, full-length animated movies, and utopian theme parks.

And how strong was this vision? After his death, at a banquet in celebration of the opening of Disney World, one of the guests turned to Disney's wife and said, "Too bad Walt never got a chance to see this." Her simple reply, "He did."

Though he didn't have a smooth ride to the top, he certainly had an interesting one. Once fired by a newspaper editor for his lack of imagination and ideas, he accepted the criticism and continued his journey. Determined to give millions a chance to share in his fertile imagination, he kept his vision in full harmony with a singleness of purpose, refusing to let anyone fill his mind with doubt.

Seventeenth-century author Jonathan Swift, known for his satirical writing, once enlightened his readers, saying, "When a true genius appears in the world, you may know him by this sign, the dunces are all in confederacy against him." Fueled by jealousy, frustration, the need to tear down, or a lack of vision, there's always someone lurking in the shadows, like a thief in the night, waiting to rob and circumvent creative genius.

As for Disney, the dunces were in confederacy against him. With bated breath, they mocked his every move. Refusing to be deterred, and with the full support of his wife, he continued to pursue a world of wishing upon stars and making all our dreams come true. Like all innovative leaders, he made his visions so clear and his convictions so deep, his doubters eventually drifted off into irrelevance, destined to wait in long lines to buy tickets to enter his magic kingdoms.

With tongue-in-cheek, it's been said, "Behind every successful man is a supportive spouse... and one very surprised mother-in-law." It's no secret, to succeed at the highest of levels and against all odds, you need support from home, and Walt Disney had it. His wife believed in him, encouraged him, was honest with him, and gave him direction. As reported in *The New York Times* by Bernard Weinraub:

> *On a train ride home after a disappointing business setback, Walt Disney talked to his wife about a new cartoon character he wanted to develop. It was a mouse, and he wanted to call it Mortimer. She didn't like the name Mortimer, saying, "It's too formal. How about Mickey?"*

And the rest is history. About ninety years of it, driven by a powerful imagination, a supportive wife, and one very surprised mother-in-law.

Like Disney, early in his career filmmaker and director Steven Spielberg was disrespected in his profession. On more than one occasion, he was rejected by the University of Southern California School of Cinematic Arts. Did he fold up his director's chair and seek a new profession? Not a chance. He went on to win numerous Academy Awards and Emmys. His first 27 movies grossed more than $9 billion dollars. Not bad for a college reject.

Sidney Poitier had a hard time getting started as an actor. During his first audition for the American Negro Theater, he flubbed his lines, delivered them with his thick Caribbean accent, and was told by the director to quit wasting his time and consider something more suitable for his talents--like washing dishes. Did he turn in his movie scripts for a washcloth and bottle of dish soap? Not a chance. He broke the color barrier in the U.S. movie industry, becoming the first African American actor to win an Academy Award. Not bad for a Caribbean speaking dishwasher.

Disney, Spielberg, and Poitier shunned their critics and stayed true to their dreams. With clear and unshakable conviction, they made a difference in the world, perhaps surprising even their mothers-in-law.

53

To lead a good life...

Check inside the belly of a Trojan horse.

Blind faith can be a dangerous thing. Before taking a leap, best put a toe in the water and check the depth before diving in.

Eager to prove our loyalty, we sometimes find ourselves, like insecure children, ready to follow the lead, without testing direction or questioning intent. The result, at breakneck speed, we find ourselves free falling into an abyss of trouble, failure, and deep regret.

It's safe to say, on June 25, 1876, General George Custer should've tested the waters before leading the 7th Calvary into the Battle of the Little Bighorn. The results of Custer's blind faith: 268 dead, 55 severely wounded. And how about the people of Troy? I'll bet they wish they would've checked inside the belly of the Trojan horse, loaded with enemy soldiers, before escorting it into the heart of their city. That night, 40 Greek warriors crept out of the 25-foot horse and opened the gates of Troy for the rest of the Greek Army. They entered the city and proceeded to destroy Troy and end the war.

In an interview, Hall of Fame baseball player Mickey Mantle tells a tale about fiery teammate Billy Martin, blindly following his lead:

> Mickey was taking Billy Martin deer hunting on a friend's land near San Antonio. Upon arrival, Mickey asked his friend if they could get started.
>
> The man said, "Yes," but asked, "When you go through the barnyard would you shoot that mule for me?"
>
> "Aw, we don't want to shoot your mule. You know, we came here to shoot deer."

"Well, you'd be doing me a big favor because I just don't have the heart. I've had him a long time. He's about twenty years old, he hasn't done any work in about ten years, and I'm going to have to have him put away anyway. If you'd shoot him for me, you'd really be doing me a big favor."

Reluctantly, Mickey agreed.

Walking back to the car, he decided to pull a joke on Billy. Yanking the car door open, he said, "Hand me my rifle. We drove four hours to get down here to go deer hunting and the guy says we can't. I'm going to shoot his mule."

Mickey takes his rifle, walks into the barnyard, and shoots the mule in the neck. As the mule hits the ground, Mickey hears a few gunshots, turns, and sees Billy standing there with smoke coming out of the barrel of his gun.

"Billy, what are you doing?"

"I got three of his cows!"

Though Billy Martin was a man of legendary loyalty, on that day, he found himself wandering the barnyard, free-falling into that abyss of deep regret. He experienced the fine line between loyalty and blind faith, realizing the first secures friendships, strengthens leadership, and solidifies a reputation of trust. The other, well, it's just flat out dangerous--dead-cow, smoking-gun dangerous.

54

To lead a good life...

Find that ax and start choppin'.

Most of us are bound and determined to make a commitment to excellence when it stops raining, gets cooler, or when the sun goes down and the mosquitoes stop biting. Right? Yeah, right.

Our noble intent is to start dieting, stop smoking, clean the closets, or dust under the bed, if not today, tomorrow for sure. And if not tomorrow, at the very latest, when all hell freezes over.

Commitment is a funny thing. It's not real complicated. We either start choppin' the wood or we pretend we can't find the ax. It isn't about words, promises, or intentions; it's about actions. With no regard for hell, high water, or when the swallows come back from Capistrano, we just gotta get up, get out of the old recliner, grab that ax, and start choppin'.

So, the next time we find ourselves ready to make a commitment to excellence, but a hangnail has us hesitating, we might want to consider the approach Alabama football coach Nick Saban presents in his book *How Good Do You Want to Be?*

> *Many centuries ago, Roman soldiers attempted to invade the island of England by attacking the cliffs of Dover. Just across the English Channel from France, the cliffs served as a close entry point for invading soldiers. But they weren't easy to climb and overtake, especially when they were being defended.*
>
> *For years the Romans tried to take the cliffs, failing, and retreating each time. They'd get into their rowboats,*

> which they launched from their ships, row to shore, and try to scale the cliffs, only to return in defeat.
> Finally, a Roman captain made a bold decision. On the next attempt, he ordered the rowboats to be burned onshore. There'd be no means of retreat. The soldiers would either succeed in taking the cliffs, or they'd perish. With no option of failure, they finally succeeded and took the cliffs.

Now, nobody's suggesting joining the Roman army, attacking the cliffs of Dover, or burning down any rowboats. But here's the humble suggestion: The next time you're faced with making a commitment to excellence, disregard any rain, fog, sleet, or hail, and don't wait for hell to freeze over or the cows to come home. You and I both know, those cows never seem to come home anyway.

If you're really serious about saving money, losing weight, exercising, or looking Mr. Wonderful in the eye to pitch a product on *Shark Tank*, you gotta row that boat right up to shore, get out, light a match, and burn it down--so to speak. As talk is cheap and promises are cheaper, you've gotta invest in yourself, believe in yourself, find that ax, swat those mosquitos, and start choppin'. Right?

One of the most dangerous jobs in America is being a commercial fisherman. It's physical work, involving fast-moving nets, slippery decks, and dangerous fishing gear. Exposed to severe weather conditions in remote areas of the world, if they get injured, there's no easy access to medical help. Being miles away from doctors, hospitals, and emergency squads, they must make a firm commitment to excellence, doing everything the right way. As fishermen are at the mercy of the open seas, their awareness, commitment, and preparation must be constant. There's little room for error or procrastination.

Imagine being a logger. Like fishing, it's physical work, involving dangerous equipment in remote areas of dense forests. They too are far away from medical assistance. Working with chainsaws, harvesters, and falling timber, their task is treacherous and unforgiving. In making decisions, they can't wait for the swallows to come back from Capistrano or the cows to come home. They must devote themselves to making timely decisions, staying attentive, and putting safety first with a no-nonsense approach at all times.

And how about heavy construction workers, bending iron, pouring concrete, or molding steel. They're often required to work with massive equipment in dangerous locations--standing high above the ground building bridges, balancing on narrow beams overlooking cities, or building roads filled with high-speed traffic. As there's a constant threat of serious injury and death, their focus and concentration must be razor-sharp at all times.

As Nick Saban would prescribe, in all group endeavors, fishing in the open seas, logging in dense forests, building highways in busy traffic, or trying to win a national championship, workers must believe in themselves, trust their co-workers, invest in the process, and get the job done. Not when it stops raining or the sun goes down, but now. It's called a commitment to excellence.

55

To lead a good life...

Don't throw water bottles.

It's often been preached, to be respected you must first respect yourself. Sounds easy, but in reality, the process can be a long, lonely, and introspective journey. Once attained, however, self-respect will unlock the heart, free the mind, and give incentive to better respect others.

Henry David Thoreau was an American essayist, poet, philosopher, and writer. His work equated to about 20 volumes of books. He was a master of putting thoughts into words. Realizing compassion is a necessary ingredient to earning respect, he asked, "Could a greater miracle take place than for us to look through each other's eyes for an instant?" Smart guy. He understood respect and compassion, and through reflective thought and unparalleled communication, he was able to express it.

In his desire to teach his football players to be respectful and compassionate of everyone in his program, a young coach taught a simple but valuable lesson to one of his players on a Friday night:

> *Calling for a time out and signaling his team to come to the sideline and take a knee, like bees to nectar, the waterboys scurried about, determined to make sure their heroes were hydrated. The young coach talked to his players, as coaches do, encouraging them to focus on reading keys, communicating, and staying fundamentally sound. When finished, the team broke the huddle and headed back onto the field of play.*

> *One player, however, didn't hand his bottle back to the waterboys. Instead, he threw it toward the sideline, forcing one of the young boys to chase it down. Not being happy with what he saw, the coach called the player back, saying, "You see that little guy? He takes as much pride in his job as you take in yours, and he thinks you walk on water. Next time he takes care of you, you look him in the eye, thank him, and hand him the water bottle. He deserves your respect. Make sure you deserve his."*

Whether singing opera, sweeping floors, running a business, or filling water bottles for a high school football team, respect and compassion matter. With typical childlike simplicity, Dr. Seuss of *The Cat in the Hat* fame, wrote, "A person's a person, no matter how small." Alice Miller, the author of *The Truth Will Set You Free*, with clarity and purpose, penned, "Disrespect is the weapon of the weak." And philosopher, writer, and Nobel Peace Prize winner Albert Schweitzer, summed up his views on respect and compassion when he said, "The purpose of human life is to serve and to show compassion and the will to help others."

A common theme is found in the thoughts of the coach and the diverse group of highly successful authors. Their message: The next time someone takes care of you, show a little compassion, and let them know you respect what they do. Chances are pretty good they deserve it, and chances are even better, it will set you free to better respect yourself.

56

To lead a good life...

Just go home and love your children.

Some people come from a homelife of support, nurturing, and love. Others come from a homelife of fear, pain, and agony. One offers a ticket to rise and accomplish. The other offers little more than busted glasses, bruises, running in the dark, and hiding in the shadows:

> *The principal called the teacher into her office and asked for help. She noticed one of the students was coming to school earlier and earlier every morning and it worried her. After talking with the little guy, she learned his father worked nights, and the boy seemed more than eager to get out of the house before his dad got home. She feared he was being abused.*
>
> *The principal told the teacher, "This morning, when I arrived, the child was standing in the cold, hiding in the shadows, waiting for the doors to open. In our conversation, he said he feels safe when you're around. Until we get this resolved, and it shouldn't take long, could you get here early and let him stay in your room as you prepare for the day?"*
>
> *The teacher agreed and arrived at school very early the next morning--about the time the custodians were ramping up the boilers and turning the hallway lights on. Opening his classroom door, he placed his books on his desk and hung up his coat. Walking back to his desk, he noticed movement in the back of the room. The little guy was already there, hiding behind a curtain. As if being*

> *hunted, he looked worried, tired, and disheveled.*
>
> *Without making eye contact, the boy asked, "Do you mind if I do my homework in your room?"*
>
> *The young student was running in the dark. He was cold, scared, and tired, yet he was worried about his homework. Tough kid. Classy kid. After about ten minutes in the classroom together, the teacher peered over the student's shoulder and was inspired by what he saw.*
>
> *"Young man, that's impressive work. Your paper is so neat and your handwriting is beautiful."*
>
> *The boy replied, "Thank you. My homeroom teacher told me if I'm neat and do all my work, maybe someday I can go away to college. I'd like that very much."*

At an early age, the young man learned to starve his pain and nourish his focus. He chose not to obsess over the trauma and hurt. He chose to zero in on his lessons, hoping to continue to grow, develop, and accomplish.

After teaching thousands of children, for over 4 decades, here's what I believe: If you want to make a difference in this confusing, fast-paced, instant gratification world of ours, go home and love your children. That's it. It's not complicated and doesn't cost much, just go home and love your children. Who knows, like the boy behind the curtain, maybe someday they'll develop the strength, the understanding, and the maturity to grow, thrive, and develop enough confidence to someday go off to college. Wouldn't that be nice?

Allow me to share with you four quotes I gathered over the years about parenting that may stimulate a touch of positive thought and action:

- Writer and homemaker Brooke Hampton wrote, "Speak to your children as though they are the wisest, kindest, most beautiful and magical people on earth, for what they believe is what they'll become."

- An anonymous source said, "Your children know you love them by your presence, not your presents."

- Best-selling author Bunmi Laditan, wrote, "If you're completely exhausted and don't know how you're going to keep giving this much of yourself day after day, you're probably a good parent."

- And another anonymous source encouraged, "Being a mother is about the strengths you didn't know you had and the fears you didn't know existed."

As though connecting an electrical circuit, direct your energy toward helping young people focus, not on the pain and hurt of neglect, but rather on their potential, giving them hope for the future. I'm sure they'd like that very much.

Review: Stories 52 - 56

52
To lead a good life... surprise even your mother-in-law.

Jonathan Swift wrote, "When a true genius appears in the world, you may know him by this sign, the dunces are all in confederacy against him." Fueled by jealousy, frustration, the need to tear down, or a lack of vision, there's always someone hiding in the shadows, waiting to rob and circumvent creative genius.

53
To lead a good life... check inside the belly of a Trojan horse.

Eager to prove our loyalty, we sometimes find ourselves ready to follow the lead, without testing direction or questioning intent. The result: we find ourselves free falling into an abyss of trouble, failure, and deep regret.

54
To lead a good life... find that ax and start choppin'.

Commitment is a funny thing. It's not real complicated. We either start choppin' the wood or we pretend we can't find the ax. It isn't about words, promises, or intentions, it's about actions.

55
To lead a good life... don't throw water bottles.

To be respected you must first respect yourself. Though the process can be a long, lonely, and introspective journey, once attained, it will unlock the heart, free the mind, and give incentive to better respect others.

56
To lead a good life... just go home and love your children.

If you want to make a difference in this confusing, fast-paced, instant gratification world of ours, take care of your family. It's not complicated and doesn't cost much, just go home, love your children, and prepare them to do the same.

57

To lead a good life...

Develop million-dollar relationships.

A wise, old philosopher once said, "If you want your relationships to look, feel, and be like a million bucks, you better treat them like they're worth a million bucks." He continued, "Anything less offers nothing more than a short-term, undervalued, promissory note."

The deep thinker understood relationships, believing those that hold their value, don't just happen. They have to grow and develop over time, with total respect for the heart, the soul, and the happiness of those involved.

Like a spring flower, when tended properly, a beauty blossoms from within a relationship, giving others a clear picture of the way it should be seeded, nurtured, cultivated, and matured. Those actions have the potential to make others crave what's been developed, giving them the incentive to grow their own relationships and the opportunity to reap the same rewards.

Keep in mind, when a challenge arises, or a devastating loss has been experienced, you won't have to face them alone. Though that person may not be able to completely fix the problem or fill the void, through an unspoken promise, those you've developed lasting relationships with, will be there for you.

The rewards of your million-dollar work may look, feel, and be something like this:

> *It was her wedding day. The radiant smile on her face as she walked down the aisle sent two, clear messages to*

the groom and everyone in attendance: I've found the right partner, and I've been blessed with the gift of a loving family.

She'd lost her father a few years earlier, but on this day, the bride and her mother wouldn't walk alone. Though her brother couldn't completely fix the problem, he could help fill the void. Together, they weathered the family storm. Together, they'd walk down the aisle. It was a powerful gesture, a beautiful picture of a million-dollar relationship, and a tribute to the strength and resilience of their family.

Another smile matched the bride's that day--her mother's. It was obvious, walking hand in hand with her son and daughter, knowing what they'd been through and how they'd persevered together, filled her with a sense of pride, validating her work as a mother and her husband's legacy as a father.

And who, you may ask, was the maid of honor? Following wedding protocol, the bride chose her best friend--her mother. For mom, there could be no greater reward. For those in attendance, it would be difficult not to crave the relationship the family had developed--the perfect message on the perfect wedding day.

Charlie and Tammy Waddington, you did good. Congratulations!

58

To lead a good life...

Quit banging your keyboard about today's troubled youth.

Read your local newspaper, surf the internet, listen to podcasts, or watch the daily news on TV, and your mind will be overloaded with the endless buzz about our troubled youth. They're mean, they're soft, they're lazy, and they're disrespectful. It's true, many have lost their way, but here's another truth: There's a bundle of good ones in this world, and they deserve some prime-time coverage, too. We're so busy pounding our keyboards about the bottom feeders, we've lost sight of those who aspire higher.

So... here it is, a little prime-time coverage for a few of the good guys:

> *The young boy pedaled his sister's bike to the stadium every day throughout the late summer and early fall. It was an old bike, rusty handlebars, tattered seat, no chain-guard, and the back rim was a bit wobbly, but it was good enough to get him to varsity football practices to help out. As the bike didn't have a kickstand anymore, he leaned it against the chain-link fence and hustled through the stadium gate.*
>
> *He loved helping the team. He was punctual, energetic, and loyal. As a low-level gofer, he filled water bottles, carried blocking bags from Point A to Point B, and made sure footballs were strategically placed around the field.*
>
> *He was a quiet kid, priding himself in being a part of*

the team, and it didn't take long for the players to appreciate his work. They respected his concern for detail and his warm appreciation for what they endured during the long, hot summer practices. The young man soaked up the team atmosphere created on the gridiron, becoming a part of who they were. He sang their songs, shared their laughter, and felt their disappointments. He was truly one of the guys.

At their end-of-the-season banquet, the captains asked the coach if they could say a few words. When their time came, they called their little buddy to the head table. He stood tall as they talked about his work ethic, his team spirit, and how much they respected him as a person. When they finished, they wheeled out a brand new bike for the little guy--a boys bike--one they purchased with their own money. It was hard to tell who was prouder, the little guy or the big kids.

The next time you find yourself in a deep, dark conversation about the sorry state of today's youth, and before you add your own fuel to the fire, remember this: Like the trusty water boy and his appreciative teammates, there are some good ones out there. Some are talented athletes, learning to work together as a team. Some are gifted musicians, methodically marching in the school band. Some are serious students, preparing to enter college or master a skilled trade, and some are just good kids, like the young boy on his new bike, riding off into the sunset, on a youthful mission to help somebody out.

I watched a young lady battle the physical and emotional strain of cancer, look death in the eye, fight back, and become a gifted speech pathologist. I coached a young man, smothered in family conflict and abuse, bounce back and start his own successful construction company. And I taught a young high school student-athlete, lost and bewildered over the death of his mother and father, lean on his faith, rebound, and become a respected educator.

Yet some misguided older folks seem obsessed with finding fault in today's youth. As if carrying megaphones, they're eager to broadcast their faults, publicize their weaknesses, and headline their failures. Perhaps more damaging, they pretend to be blessed with all the right answers, and with a sly little wink and a clever little smile, they'll mock anyone who believes otherwise. Sadly, they're unable to fathom the idea our youth are kind enough, creative enough, and resourceful enough to buy and present a new bike to a hard-working waterboy... but they are.

So there it is, a little prime-time coverage for a few of the good guys.

59

To lead a good life…

Get up on the table and sing your song.

Ever notice, solid leaders believe in a cause and they're not afraid to show it. Their vision is so strong, their conviction is so deep, and their desire to make a difference is so powerful, like an A student, when called upon to meet their challenges and represent, they find their voice, move to the head of the class, and motivate.

How about the first person to ask, "Hey, what do you guys say we try to land on the moon? Huh, what do you think? Maybe we can even get a car up there and drive around a bit. You know, pick up some moon rocks, get back in the spacecraft, cruise on home, and check 'em out. What do you think? You guys in or what? It'd be like taking one small step for man, and a big ole leap for mankind. Would that be cool or what?"

Do you suppose that person, in his desire to rally his buddies to support the cause, was timid and shy in his approach? Come on, you know the guy had to have a fire in his belly strong enough to launch a few long-range, guided missiles.

To motivate people to reach for the stars, in any endeavor, there has to be a fearlessness evolve from within the group. As indicated below, there has to be someone strong enough, bold enough, maybe even crazy enough, to inspire others to come together, stay together, and get the job done:

> *At a small college in the midwest, as a rite of passage--and to send a message about the value of school spirit--*

it was a tradition for each freshmen football player to sing their high school fight song in front of the entire team. Like sheep to be sheared, they lined up and quietly waited their turn. If a young man didn't represent his alma mater with pride, the veterans hooted and hollered at the poor soul, playfully shaming him for his lack of school spirit.

One year a freshman, just back from a tour of duty overseas, wasn't about to shy away from anybody or anything. He learned about pride and tradition in high school, competing against rival teams, and in the army, fighting for his country. When his name was called to sing, he didn't hesitate.

With complete confidence, he leaped up on one of the cafeteria tables and sang his heart out, making direct eye contact with every upperclassman in the room. Upon finishing, he jumped down, waited for the standing ovation to die down, and said, "Now, I'm not sure what these other fools were singing, but I was singing my high school fight song, the way it's supposed to be sung because I'm proud of my school." And oh, how the next players sang!

The next time you stop believing in miracles, look up at the moon and envision a man, about 239,000 miles away, riding in a little car upon its surface, and understand this: For miracles to happen, of the humankind, the ride on the moon kind, like the veteran jumping up on the table to sing his song, there has to be someone bold enough to motivate others to come together, to stay together, and to see the miracle through. And oh, how the others will follow!

60

To lead a good life...

Put down the quill pen and serve others.

The professor fixed his glasses, adjusted his tie, and continued his lecture on servant leadership, saying, "People of a shallow existence determine greatness by the number serving them. Others, of a deeper, more honorable stature, determine theirs by the number they serve." Powerful statement.

His overall message was clear. Dedicating ourselves to others prepares us for leadership and ensures a more cooperative existence. Keeping that in mind, if we want people to follow our lead, we should spend more time teaching, preaching, and role-modeling servant leadership.

The professor's final thought, "In lifting others, we elevate ourselves, enhancing our own chances of achieving, succeeding, and finding happiness."

By the professor's standards, servant leadership might look something like this:

> *His nickname was "Woody." He was a tremendous local sports fan. Suffering from a muscular disease, he wasn't able to participate in athletics throughout his childhood. With enthusiasm and intense pride, he funneled his love of competition into cheering for and supporting his hometown teams. Everybody loved Woody, you couldn't help but admire his spirit and enthusiasm.*
>
> *As the disease robbed him of much of his independence, it was customary for a couple of high*

> *school basketball players to stop by his house and take him to home games. On this night, as other ballplayers had done so often in the past, two players carried him into the gym, across the hardwood floor, and eased him onto the bleachers. Making sure he was comfortable, they headed back across the floor to prepare for the game.*
>
> *As they neared the locker room, their coach called them over, saying, "Nothing you do tonight, scoring points, grabbing rebounds, or winning this game, will be more impressive than the way you just took care of Woody."*

Here's the beauty of greatness, and ya' gotta love it: You don't need to grab a chisel and sculpt like Michelangelo, pound the keys of a piano-like Frederic Chopin, write with a quill pen-like Leo Tolstoy, or sing opera like Luciano Pavarotti. Nope. 'Bout all ya' gotta do is serve others.

And here's the beauty of service: You don't need a high IQ, a college degree, or a skilled trade to make it happen. You don't need to know how to conjugate verbs, solve algebraic expressions, or memorize the periodic table of elements. All you need is enough compassion to carry a young man across a gym floor, ease him down on a set of bleachers, and make sure he's comfortable. That's it!

61

To lead a good life...

Wear your coonskin cap with pride.

Pressure from your peers is one of the strongest forces known to man. As though diving for lost treasure, people search for the strength and resolve to handle peer pressure.

Here's a lesson from a ten-year-old student on a mission to send a powerful message of strength and resolve to his peers:

The young student was king of the wild frontier... for about two hours. Walking down the hall, he puffed his chest out and cracked an all-knowing smile. He was wearing his brand new, Davy Crockett coonskin cap, and he was in pioneer heaven.

Some of the boys in his class flocked to get a glimpse of his cap, marveling at its authenticity and natural, raccoon beauty. Word spread like a Kansas prairie fire, and some of the boys weren't too keen about the attention the Davy Crockett look-alike was receiving. They decided to ambush him out on the playground, test his wrestling skills, steel his coonskin cap, and wipe that trend-setting grin off his face.

Ganging up on the young trailblazer, the jealous rascals played keep-away with his beloved hat. Grappling hard, he stood his ground and finally recaptured his prized possession. With hat in hand, he hightailed it back into the building and buried it deep in his locker.

Sweating like a fifteen-round boxer, he wiped his brow and returned to his classroom a bit early. The teacher could see the young man was agitated and asked what happened.

"Some of the boys in our class stole my coonskin cap."

"Why'd they do that?"

"I think they're jealous. It's a beauty... and the girls really like it."

"So where's the cap now?"

"I got it back. It's in my locker. Do you think I could wear it during class? I want to show them I'm not backing down."

"Sure, go get it."

Sitting at his desk, young Crockett was shaking and breathing like a rabid dog. With jutted jaws and clenched fists, he was peering at the door, waiting for the good-old-boys to come back into the room.

With his recaptured coonskin cap on his head and its tail dangling over his shoulder, he was ready to show those scoundrels conspiring against him they were picking on the wrong woodsman.

As they came in, the boys noticed his cap, his demeanor, and his steadfast refusal to be intimidated. The message was Windex clear, he was wearing his coonskin cap, and he wasn't bowing down to their mob mentality.

When peer pressure starts to rear its ugly head, I doubt you'll have to wrestle on the ground to recapture a coonskin cap, but you will be tested. Though you may lose a few friends along the way and experience some sleepless nights, in refusing to back down, like the Davy Crockett look-alike, your integrity will be intact and you'll send those fools conspiring against you a message of your toughness and resolve.

62

To lead a good life...

Trust that the sky is no longer the limit.

Helen Keller once said, and she would know better than most, "The only thing worse than being blind is having sight but no vision." Though creative vision is a necessary component of accomplishment, there has to be more to the story. As a Japanese proverb assures, "Vision without action is a daydream. Action, without vision, is a nightmare."

Thomas Jefferson had a vision. He wanted to help create a document to insure freedom from religious oppression, injustice, and disrespect for human rights. He didn't just dream it. He acted upon it, and his actions are evident in his draft of the Declaration of Independence.

Michelangelo had a vision. His desire to create a work of art, capturing the human drama of the death of Christ, wasn't just an idea. He took action, chiseling his vision in gray marble and calling it the Pieta.

How about William Shakespeare? He had a vision. He didn't just dream of mastering the art of writing. He put pen to paper and for centuries his poetry and plays have had a profound impact on the culture of the world.

In *Developing the Leader Within You*, author John C. Maxwell shares a passage about putting vision into action:

> *A bishop from the East Coast visited a small Midwestern religious college. He stayed at the home of*

> *the college president who served as a professor of physics and chemistry. After dinner, the bishop declared that the millennium couldn't be far off because just about everything in nature had been discovered and all inventions conceived.*
>
> *The young college president politely disagreed and said he felt there would be many more discoveries. When the enraged bishop challenged the president to name just one such invention, the president replied he was certain that within fifty years men would be able to fly.*
>
> *"Nonsense!" sputtered the outraged bishop, "Only angels are intended to fly."*
>
> *The bishops' name was Wright. He had two boys at home who would prove to have a greater vision than their father. You've heard of them. Their names were Orville and Wilbur, American inventors and pioneers of aviation. The father and his sons both lived under the same sky, but they had different horizons.*

As proven from the white sands of Kitty Hawk to the gray powder on the moon, the sky is no longer the limit. Putting thoughts and words into action, the only real limit to accomplishment is found in the mind.

Shakespeare and Jefferson started with nothing more than a blank piece of parchment paper, and Michelangelo started with a single block of Carrara marble. Being cut from the same cloth, the Wright Brothers, with a spool of wire, a bundle of wooden slats, and a handful of used bicycle parts, followed their lead. For them, there'd be no daydreaming, no nightmares, and no worries about doubting bishops spewing outrage--just strong visions and plenty of action.

57
To lead a good life... develop million-dollar relationships.
When tended properly, a beauty blossoms from within a relationship, giving others a clear picture of the way it should be seeded, nurtured, cultivated, and matured. Those actions have the potential to make others crave what's been developed.

58
To lead a good life... quit banging your keyboard about today's troubled youth.
There's an endless buzz about today's troubled youth. They're mean, they're soft, they're lazy, and they're disrespectful. It's true, many have lost their way, but here's another truth: There's a bundle of good ones in this world, and they deserve some prime-time coverage, too.

59
To lead a good life... get up on the table and sing your song.
To motivate people to reach for the stars, in any endeavor, there has to be a fearlessness evolve from within the group.

60
To lead a good life... put down the quill pen and serve others.
Dedicating ourselves to others prepares us for leadership and ensures a more cooperative existence. If we want people to follow our lead, we should spend more time teaching, preaching, and role-modeling servant leadership.

61
To lead a good life... wear your coonskin cap with pride.
When peer pressure starts to rear its ugly head, you will be tested. Though you may lose a few friends along the way and experience some sleepless nights, in refusing to back down, your integrity will be intact and you'll send those fools conspiring against you a message of your toughness and refusal to back down.

62

To lead a good life... trust that the sky is no longer the limit.

As proven from the white sands of Kitty Hawk to the gray powder on the moon, the sky is no longer the limit. Putting thoughts and words into action, the only real limit to accomplishment is found in the mind.

Suggested Reading to Help Inspire, Motivate, and Lead

LEAD... for God'Sake!--A Parable for Finding the Heart of Leadership by Todd Gongwer.

"This book is a book I could not put down until I finished it. Every parent, coach, manager, and leader should read it. I wish I had read it 30 years ago."--Lou Holtz, legendary college football coach.

The Heart of a Leader--Insights on the Art of Influence, by Ken Blanchard.

"Ken Blanchard is one of America's best-known leadership and business experts. And now he helps you understand and experience the art of influence by revealing the greatest life and leadership lessons he's learned in his rich career as an educator and business leader."--As written on the jacket of his book.

The Heart of a Teacher--A Treasury of Inspiration by Paula Fox.

"If you're a teacher; or if, like me, your life was greatly influenced by a teacher... you're going to love this book! The inspirational stories, the photographs, the quotes, and Paula Fox's beautiful, original poems will find a special place in your heart."--Mac Anderson, founder of *Simple Truths*.

The 21 Irrefutable Laws of Leadership--Follow Them and People Will Follow You by John C. Maxwell.

"If you've never read *The 21 Irrefutable Laws of Leadership*, you've been missing out on one of the best leadership books of all time."--As written on the jacket of his book.

How Good Do You Want to Be?--A Champion's Tips on How to Lead and Succeed at Work and in Life by Nick Saban with Brian Curtis

"The winning philosophy for creating and inspiring success from the hottest football coach in the game: Nick Saban."--As written on the jacket of his book.

The Art of War by Sun Tzu, Translated by Thomas Cleary.

"Thomas Cleary's translation of Sun Tzu's 2,000-year-old *The Art of War* makes immediately relevant one of the greatest Chinese classical texts. There's not a dated maxim or vague prescription in it. 'To win without fighting is best,' Sun Tzu said. For him, war was coeval with life. Absorb this book, and you can throw out all those contemporary books about management leadership."--*Newsweek*

Leaders Eat Last --Why Some Teams Pull Together and Others Don't by Simon Sinek.

"Leaders are the ones who run headfirst into the unknown. They rush toward the danger. They put their own interests aside to protect us or to pull us into the future. Leaders would sooner sacrifice what is theirs to save what is ours. And they would never sacrifice what is ours to save what is theirs."--As written on the jacket of his book.

God Never Blinks--50 Lessons for Life's Little Detours by Regina Brett.

"Regina Brett is a gifted observer of the experiences that shape who we are, and her lessons unfold with buoyancy, humor, and courageous honesty. She has given us a beautifully written road map for life."-- Jefferey Zaslow, coauthor of *The Last Lecture.*

What Makes the Great Great--Strategies for Extraordinary Achievement by Dennis P. Kimbro, Ph.D.

"Like an Olympic torch, this brilliant rekindling of timeless truth can lead a generation frustrated by discrimination and its resulting self-doubt out of a vicious circle and into the 'victors circle." I have always believed that true wealth is an internal quality and that real success is color-blind. Dennis Kimbro has reignited this wisdom for all of us to share at a time when none of us can afford to drop the baton."--Author of *The Psychology of Winning*, Dennis Waitley

Hand Me Another Brick--Timeless Lessons in Leadership, How Effective Leaders Motivate Themselves and Others by Charles R. Swindoll.

"Charles Swindoll brings his sensible and straightforward style to offer a deeply spiritual approach to the role of leader. Whatever the context, secular or ministerial, he demonstrates how to size up a task, organize and motivate a team, and respond to inevitable obstacles.... "-- As written on the back of his book.

The Everyday I Ching--or Book of Changes by Sarah Denning.

"The *I Ching* is NOT a book of fortune-telling. Nor is it a substitute for your own common sense. It is meant for giving guidance in situations where you are uncertain about the best direction to take. Use it well and it will enhance your life as though it were a wise and trusted friend."--As written in the introduction of her book.

Outliers--The Story of Success by Malcolm Gladwell.

"Gladwell's theories could be used to run a business more effectively, to turn products into runaway bestsellers, and perhaps most important, to alter human behavior."--*New York Times*

***Make Your Bed--Little Things That Can Change Your Life... and Maybe the World* by Admiral William H. McRaven (U.S. Navy Retired).**

"If you make your bed every morning, you will have accomplished the first task of the day. It will give you a small sense of pride and it will encourage you to do another task and another. By the end of the day, that one task completed will have turned into many tasks completed. Making your bed will also reinforce the fact that little things in life matter. If you can't do the little things right, you will never do the big things right."-- From Admiral McRaven's University of Texas commencement speech.

***Good to Great--Why Some Companies Make the Leap... and Others Don't* by Jim Collins.**

"The carefully researched and well-written book disproves most of the current management hype--from the cult of the superhuman CEO to the cult of IT to the acquisitions and merger mania. It will not enable mediocrity to become competence. But it should enable competence to become excellence."--Peter F. Drucker, management consultant, educator, and author.

***My Personal Best--Life Lessons from an All-American Journey* by John Wooden with Steve Jamison.**

"Read this book! Legends like Coach John Wooden don't just come out of nothing. Meet the man from the beginning--his family, his struggles, his triumphs, his character development, and his earned wisdom. If you want to learn how to win, to really consistently win in life, read this book.--Dr. Stephen Covey, author, *The 7 Habits of Highly Effective People.*

***Uncommon--Finding Your Path to Significance* by Tony Dungy with Nathan Whitaker.**

"When Indianapolis Colts coach Tony Dungy took home the trophy in Super Bowl XLI, fans around the world looked to him as the epitome of success. Athletic victory, professional excellence, fame and celebrity, awards and honor... he had it all. But even at that moment, Tony Dungy knew that those achievements had little to do with his ultimate significance as a man."--As written on the back of his book.

***That's Why I'm Here--The Chris and Stefanie Spielman Story* by Chris Spielman with Bruce Covey.**

"A powerful story for anyone whose life has been touched by cancer... and for anyone whose faith has wavered in the face of adversity. *That's Why I'm Here* is an inspiring memoir of Ohio State football legend, NFL All-Pro player, and ESPN college football analyst Chris Spielman and his wife Stefaine--a story of family, faith, and perseverance.

Author's Note

Dear Reader,

Thank you for buying To Lead a Good Life.... I hope the stories written guide you in your quest to lead, motivate, and inspire. I feel confident the lessons learned will help you aspire higher and reach your maximum potential--resulting in a happier, more prosperous life.

I would also encourage you to share this book with family, friends, and people you are charged to lead. I feel confident each story has the potential to bring you, your loved ones, your friends, and your co-workers together to better appreciate and navigate life's journeys.

As I am in the process of writing another self-help book, feel free to send me inspirational stories that have touched your life at legandot@gmail.com.

Yours in leading a good life,

Tony Legando

About the Author

Tony Legando was born in Huron, Ohio. He graduated from Huron High School and received a Bachelor of Science in Education Degree from Ashland University. He taught elementary school for 40 years, was the head football coach at Huron High School for 28 years, and is a member of the Ohio High School Football Coaches Hall of Fame.

Tony is a team-building specialist who has influenced leaders throughout his professional career and has taken his passion to mentor, impact, and facilitate on the road as a motivational speaker. He also writes a column in the *Sandusky Register* and the *Norwalk Reflector* on leadership, motivation, and inspiration.

This is his first book.

He lives in Huron with his wife Sandy, has two children, Tony and Jessie, and two granddaughters, Rece and Layne Gimperling.

His website is www.tonylegando.com and his email address is legandot@gmail.com.